HOW TO WITNESS SUCCESSFULLY

Other Books by Dr. George Sweeting

How to Begin the Christian Life
Love Is The Greatest
Living in a Dying World
How to Solve Conflicts
Discovering the Will of God
Special Sermons for Special Days

HOW TO WITNESS

SUCCESSFULLY

*A Guide for Christians
to Share the Good News*

GEORGE SWEETING

58377

MOODY PRESS

CHICAGO

Dedicated to
Mary Irving Sweeting
a saintly mother who was a
true witness of Jesus Christ.

©1978 by
THE MOODY BIBLE INSTITUTE
OF CHICAGO

Library of Congress Cataloging in Publication Data

Sweeting, George, 1924-
  How to witness successfully

  Includes bibliographical references.
  1. Witness bearing (Christianity) I. Title.
BV4520.S93   248'.5   78-1959
ISBN 0-8024-3797-4

Printed in the United States of America

Contents

HOW TO USE THIS BOOK

1. *Read it alone.* This book is designed to assist you in a personal, spiritual preparation for sharing your faith. To be successful in witnessing, you must be totally committed to the task. Do not rush through the material. Study it carefully day by day and let the Holy Spirit work in and through you as you apply what you read.
2. *Study it with a friend.* Our Lord's pattern for evangelism in Luke 10 was to send out the seventy two by two, "into every city and place" (Luke 10:1). It can be very rewarding to study and interact with a friend and then to put these principles into practice in team witnessing.
3. *Use it in a group study.* The thirteen lessons found in this book can easily be adapted for use in your Sunday school curriculum. A class on personal witnessing could do wonders for your church's visitation program.

PREFACE

Each generation is only one generation away from the eclipse of the Christian faith. That means we are responsible to reach our own generation. In this book I share Bible principles and personal experiences related to reaching our world through witnessing. Although I have more to learn, I have included many of the things God is teaching me. Witnessing, to some, is a frightening experience, even though our responsibility is spelled out in the Bible. Let me assure you—you *can* witness successfully. The information in this book has been shared personally and publicly with enthusiastic response. It is offered to you with love and the hope that you will be encouraged to witness successfully.

I determined that as I loved Christ, and as Christ loved souls, I would press Christ on the individual soul, so that none who were in the proper sphere of my individual responsibility or influence should lack the opportunity of meeting the question whether or not they would individually trust and follow Christ. The resolve I made was, that whenever I was in such intimacy with a soul as to be justified in choosing my subject of conversation, the theme of themes should have prominence between us, so that I might learn his need, and, if possible, meet it.

That decision has largely shaped my Christian life-work in the half-century that has followed its making.

Henry Clay Trumbull, in
Individual Work for Individuals

Consider the ministry of our Lord Jesus Himself. He was a man who constantly answered questions. But someone will say, "Didn't He say that to be saved you have to be as a little child?" Of course, He did. But did you ever see a little child who didn't ask questions? . . .

Christianity demands that we have enough compassion to learn the questions of our generation.

Francis Schaeffer, at
an international congress
on world evangelization

1

HOW I BEGAN TO WITNESS

As a teenager, I came alive to my Christian responsibilities on August 16, 1941. A verse of Scripture grabbed me with such force that I could never be the same. The verse was, "Be ye doers of the word, and not hearers only, deceiving your own selves" (James 1:22). Although I knew the teachings of the Bible, I had failed to obey the truth I professed to believe. That day I promised the Lord that I would be a "doer of the word."

Ordinarily I would hesitate to begin a book with a personal experience. And yet I want to be open to you so you can sense my spiritual pulse. What God did for me, He is ready, able, and anxious to do for you.

SALVATION

Of course, the starting point in the romance of witnessing is the new birth. Without it we are spiritually dead, and dead things cannot grow or multiply. Witnessing is sharing the new life that is in Jesus Christ, and it is impossible to share something that we do not have. Unless we know Jesus Christ personally and are partakers of His life, we cannot talk about Him or witness to others.

It is possible to say the right things about Christ, or tell the gospel, or quote Bible verses; but sharing about Christ and sharing Christ are two different things. Insincerity or uncertainty will cause you to be unsuccessful. You must have that inner assurance that you have received God's salvation.

I confessed my faith in Jesus Christ while still a boy. To the best of my ability, I opened my life to Christ. But like so many others, I was selfish, and rebellious to the teaching of Scripture. Ego was king in my life. I had my own plans and was determined to see them through.

That August over three decades ago, in a special church meeting, I agreed to do the will of God. I vividly recall that I had a strong urge to be alone where I could talk and listen to God and seek whatever plan He might have for me. I spent a few minutes with the pastor, talking about God's will for my life.

To get to my home meant a bus ride of at least ten miles and an additional three-mile walk. The ride and walk were different that night as I felt carried along by the thrill and excitement of my decision. That bus ride and walk gave me time alone with God.

My mother was the kind of person who never went to bed until all of her six children were home and settled in bed. That night she seemed intuitively to understand that something important and beautiful had taken place in my life. She shared warmly about the things of God and then committed me to the Lord's care.

My bedroom was a small, unheated area of our house that once had been an attic. That night in my room, as I knelt alone in prayer, I wrote down some goals. Although I was an average teenager, four goals came to mind that have intensified over the passing years. They are:

1. Seek, above everything else, to bring glory to God (1 Corinthians 10:31).
2. Cultivate the inner life (2 Peter 3:18).
3. Disciple as many people as possible (Matthew 28:19, 20).
4. Win as many people to Jesus Christ as possible (Proverbs 11:30).

Today, thirty years later, those are still my goals.

As I knelt, aglow with love and enthusiasm, I vowed a vow to be a witness. My commitment was total.

Immediately, I began to share the good news with my school friends. Most, like Paul, who sat next to me in mechanical drawing class, were not Christians. He was a likable person, and I was concerned about his spiritual welfare. Where would I start? How would I begin the conversation? What would he think of me? What would I say if he showed interest? Those were just a few of the questions racing through my mind.

INSTRUCTION

I was privileged to grow up in a church where we enjoyed a loving Bible-teaching ministry. Our pastor's sermons were helpful, and he was sensitive to our needs. He avoided excesses. He and his spiritually minded lay people were continually sharing Christ and encouraging the young people to do the same. We were so well-grounded concerning the person and work of Christ that our witnessing was the natural overflow of a personal relationship.

The young people and our sponsors formed a group to conduct services in missions, churches, hospitals, jails, and wherever people would let us share the Good News. That not only deepened our commitment to Christ, but also provided continual opportunities for us to learn by experience how to witness.

One of the suggestions recommended to start a conversation was the use of appealing literature. The first booklet I used was *Safety, Certainty and Enjoyment,* by George Cutting. Equipped with a few copies, I went off to school seeking God's guidance. I'll never forget my very first try. "Paul," I said, "here's a booklet that means a lot to me. I'd like you to read it and tell me tomorrow what you think of it." Paul took the booklet and promised to read it. I was afraid, and it was a weak start, but it was a start.

The booklet begins by stating,

11

You are traveling—traveling from time into eternity. And who knows how near you may be this moment to the Great Terminus? Let me ask you then, "What class are you traveling?" There are just three.

First class—those who are saved and know it.

Second class—those who are not sure of salvation but anxious to be so.

Third class—those who are not only unsaved but totally indifferent about it.

The next day, Paul told me that he was in the second class, not sure of salvation but anxious to be so. Being shy and fearful, I invited Paul to my home after school where I could at least attempt to answer his questions in privacy. Fear is normal and universal. I was fearful for three reasons. First, I was afraid of being personally rejected or ridiculed. Second, I was fearful that Jesus would be rejected because of me. And third, I feared that he might be so unimpressed as to consider neither of us worth rejecting.

APPLICATION

Because I was a young Christian, I witnessed with simple, understandable words. I still believe that a good policy in witnessing is to keep the presentation simple. Words like *redemption* and *propitiation* are great words, but not for witnessing. Sick souls need simple words.

Witnessing, of course, includes more than rattling off verses of Scripture. It includes *what I am* and *what I do* as well as *what I say*. It involves sharing "who Jesus Christ is" and "what Jesus has done." It is telling people that Jesus Christ is the sinless Son of God who died for the sins of the world and that He arose from the grave and wants to be involved in their daily lives.

In my stumbling way, I told Paul all I knew about Jesus. To the best of my ability, I presented the plan of salvation from the Bible, using familiar passages of Scripture.

First, I showed Paul the spiritual condition of the whole human race. We read Romans 3:23, "For all have sinned, and come short of the glory of God." I then turned to Isaiah 53:6, "All we like sheep have gone astray; we have turned every one to his own way; and the LORD hath laid on him the iniquity of us all."

Second, I explained who Jesus was, and what He did. Together we read John 14:6, "Jesus saith unto him, I am the way, the truth, and the life: no man cometh unto the Father, but by me." That was followed by reading John 3:16, "For God so loved the world, that he gave his only begotten Son, that whosoever believeth in him should not perish, but have everlasting life."

Third, I talked about what it is to repent of sin and believe in Jesus Christ. We looked at the words of Peter in Acts 3:19, "Repent ye therefore, and be converted, that your sins may be blotted out."

The Scripture did its work, and Paul was ready to receive Jesus Christ. Simply and beautifully, he welcomed Christ into his life and became a child of God. That happy day will forever live in my memory.

Over the years I have seen Paul as he has grown spiritually. In spite of my timidity, youth, and lack of knowledge, God used that simple witness. Paul was the first of more than forty classmates that I had the thrill of pointing to Christ. In fact, some of the children of my spiritual children are students at the Moody Bible Institute today.

EVANGELIZATION

The first instructions of Jesus to His followers were, "Come . . . after me, and I will make you to become fishers of men" (Mark 1:17). His last instructions while on earth to His disciples were, "But ye shall receive power, after that the Holy Ghost is come upon you: and ye shall be witnesses unto me both in Jerusalem, and in all Judea, and in Samaria, and unto the uttermost part of the earth" (Acts 1:8). Jesus began and finished His earthly ministry with the command to be witnesses.

Will Houghton used to say, "Our only excuse for living is to be a witness." Our supreme purpose in life is to bring glory to God. Spirit-filled witnessing accomplishes that purpose. When Moses went to Pharaoh, he asked, "Let my people go, that they may serve me" (Exodus 9:1). The Lord freed His ancient people so that they could serve Him. The motto is true, "We are saved to serve." Remember this: each believer in Jesus Christ is under divine orders to share the gospel with the whole world. And yet, while stressing that fact, we must remember that our abilities to witness differ. We dare not let that become an excuse for not witnessing, but rather a challenge to develop fully our God-given gifts, some of which may be still undiscovered.

It is also essential that each of us give himself to people, so that he can sense and feel their needs. Each individual is different and must always be approached with an understanding of his individuality.

Here are a few more suggestions:

Prepare a list of some friends who need to know Christ.

Pray for them each day.

Attempt to become involved with them in some type of activity.

Seek to reflect Christ in acts of kindness.

Share some attractive Christian literature.

Tactfully share what Jesus Christ means to you and how they can experience the forgiveness of sins.

Somewhere in your witnessing, you will want to invite and accompany your friends to church.

Remember, too, that God in His grace is ready and able to use each of us as he is. In God's strength, you can be a successful witness.

It is very difficult to steer a parked car, so may I urge you to get moving. Start where you are, with what you have, but start. The best way to begin is to begin, and the best time to begin is now!

REMINDERS

• Witnessing is sharing all about Jesus Christ.

- No one can witness concerning Jesus Christ success-fully until he has been converted.
- Each believer in Jesus Christ is under direct orders to share the gospel with the whole world.
- It is very difficult to steer a parked car. May I urge you to begin moving.

QUESTIONS

1. What is the starting point in all witnessing?
2. What does witnessing involve?
3. Write the first and last instructions of Jesus to His disciples.
4. What are some ways a church can encourage its people to witness?
5. Select at least three choice tracts or booklets that could be used to introduce a witnessing situation.
6. Memorize the following verses: Romans 3:23; Isaiah 53:6; John 14:6; John 3:16; Acts 3:19; Mark 1:17; and Acts 1:8.

Always use your Bible in personal dealing. Do not trust to memory, but make the person read the verse for himself. Do not use printed slips or books. Hence, if convenient, always carry a Bible or New Testament with you. . . .

Sometimes a few minutes in prayer have done more for a man than two hours in talk. . . .

Urge an immediate decision, but never tell a man he is converted. . . . Let the Holy Spirit reveal that to him. . . .

Always be prepared to do personal work. . . .

Do the work boldly. Don't take those in a position in life above your own, but, as a rule, take those on the same footing. Don't deal with a person of the opposite sex if it can be otherwise arranged. Bend all your endeavors to answer for poor, struggling souls that question of such importance to them, "What must I do to be saved?"

D. L. Moody, quoted in
The Life of D. L. Moody, by W. R. Moody

2

HOW TO PREPARE TO WITNESS

This chapter is all about you and your preparation. Each of us has opportunities, but it is the prepared witness who makes the most of them. Consider the three areas of spiritual, mental, and physical preparation.

SPIRITUAL PREPARATION

To be a successful witness, one must possess:

The Assurance of Salvation

Jesus said, "We speak that which we do know, and testify that we have seen" (John 3:11). In other words, we know what we are talking about. A living, personal experience of salvation is where we all begin. The greater our assurance, the better our witness. An uncertain salvation has little or no appeal. The doubter convinces no one. If you are not sure you are a Christian, review the promises of God and settle the matter right now.

A Consistent Christian Life

Although God in His sovereignty can use anything, He prefers to use a dedicated person. The Old Testament tells how God used a lowly ass to speak His word, and the New Testament reminds us how Peter was rebuked by a crowing cock. Sometimes God takes a crooked stick and makes a straight lick. Yet, just as a surgeon is cautious about the instruments he uses, so is God. Clean hands and a pure heart are important assets in witnessing. God does not require a beautiful vessel for witnessing, but He does demand a clean one (Romans 12:1, 2).

A Love for People

God loves people and so must we. Jesus continually revealed His compassion for people. His loving heart was wide open as He saw people groping in confusion. Jesus said, "Love one another as I have loved you." He displayed that love at Bethlehem and Calvary. He loves and cares, and we must do the same.

Our witnessing is to be loving. To rattle off Bible verses mechanically with the hope of discharging our spiritual responsibility is a farce. Love cares deeply. Love gets involved. Love communicates.

Persistent Prayer

Before we speak to people about God, it is imperative that we speak to God about people. God honors prayer. We should ask the Lord to lead us to the right person, give us the right words, and enable us to make the right approach. Prayer is an essential part of our spiritual preparation and must support every effort.

Perseverance

In the account of the Ethiopian in Acts 8, the Spirit of God said to Philip, "Go join thyself to this chariot." The Greek word for "join" really means "glue." Go and stick to that person. We need persistence and determination if we are to witness successfully. And yet even our determination must be balanced with love and good sense.

Dependence on the Holy Spirit

Before His ascension, Jesus said, "Go ye therefore, and teach all nations, baptizing them in the name of the Father, and of the Son, and of the Holy Ghost: Teaching them to observe all things whatsoever I have commanded you: and, lo, I am with you alway, even unto the end of the world" (Matthew 28:19, 20). That is the staggering promise of His abiding presence with soul winners. Christ in-dwells every believer through the Holy Spirit. The greater our understanding and appropriation of God the Holy Spirit, the greater will be our success in witnessing. We may share to perfection, but only the Holy Spirit convicts of sin.

Charles Haddon Spurgeon said that a successful wit-ness must have holiness of character, spiritual life to a high degree, humility of spirit, a living faith, a thorough earnestness, great simplicity of heart, and a complete sur-render to God. Spurgeon had those qualities, and God used him in a special way to win many to eternal life.

MENTAL PREPARATION

Spiritual preparation is, of course, foundational to wit-nessing. But another important—even vital—area of preparation is mental preparation. The successful wit-ness is mentally prepared. Mental preparation for wit-nessing involves knowing the Scriptures, understanding the gospel, having the right attitude, and being at ease.

Know the Scriptures

The Bible is God's instrument in saving people. Always remember, the Word of God is quick and powerful. It is the sword of the Spirit. The more we understand the truths of the Bible, the greater will be our success. There is no authority like the Bible. R. A. Torrey wrote:

> A practical knowledge of the Bible involves four things:
>
> 1. A knowledge how to so use the Bible as to show men, and make men realize, their need of a Saviour.
>
> 2. A knowledge of how to use the Bible so as to show men Jesus as just the Saviour who meets their need.
>
> 3. A knowledge of how to use the Bible so as to show men how to make Jesus their own Saviour.
>
> 4. A knowledge of how to use the Bible so as to meet the difficulties that stand in the way of their accepting Christ.[1]

---

[1] R. A. Torrey, *How to Work for Christ* (Chicago: Revell, 1901), p. 25.

A knowledge of the Bible is essential if we are to witness successfully.

Understand the Gospel

Basic as it may seem, a thorough understanding of the gospel is often overlooked as a prerequisite for witnessing. To be a successful witness, one must understand and know how to explain clearly and concisely such fundamental doctrines as the sinfulness of man, the righteousness of God, the principle of atonement, and the relationship of grace and works.

Have the Right Attitude

Recently I was flying to Washington, D.C. The businessman sitting next to me offered me a drink of vodka. In a friendly, natural way I simply said, "No, thank you."

A few minutes later, he noticed my Bible and said, "You seem to be religious, and I guess you think I'm ugly." "No," I responded, "I think you're a very generous person." Immediately he was receptive, and I tactfully shared the gospel with him.

I could easily have answered, "No, thank you, I'm a Christian." In all likelihood he would have felt I was putting him down, and the door of opportunity would have been closed.

Be prepared to respond carefully and wisely to profanity, off-color stories, or drinking. Although we oppose the life-style of some, we must always, always, love the individual. Careful preparation can avoid trouble spots. Too often we are unprepared and respond in such a way as to broaden the gap. Paul Little felt that our preparation should include being ready to make a positive contribution to awkward situations. "Every Christian," he said, "should always have five sure-fire jokes at his disposal. Well chosen, well-timed humor can reset the whole tone of a conversation; it can carry you over a seemingly impossible hurdle. Like remembering names, the only way to remember a joke is to use it immediately after you hear it. If necessary, write it down afterwards. Then tell it whenever you get a chance."[2] There's no doubt about it, a wholesome, humorous story can rescue an awkward situation.

It is helpful to ask the person to whom you are witnessing for permission to share concerning spiritual things.

Be prepared to use your testimony. I would strongly encourage you to write out how you came to know Jesus Christ and what He means to you. Your testimony should be carefully prepared and memorized so that at a moment's notice you are ready to take three to five minutes to relate the gospel. Whatever you do, be sensitive and tactful.

Tact has been defined as the right touch rather than the wrong touch. We are instructed in Scripture to let our lights shine, but remember—not like a blow torch! J. Oswald Sanders defines tact as "an intuitive perception of what is proper or fitting; the mental ability of saying and doing the right thing at the right time, so as not to unnecessarily offend or anger. This qualification is sadly often conspicuous by its absence and the worker spoils the very work about which he is so concerned."[3]

Acts 16 tells the conversion experiences of at least two people. One of them, Lydia, listened quietly and then in a matter-of-fact way opened her life to Christ; whereas the other, the jailer, experienced a sudden, dramatic, emotional conversion.

Some come to Christ quietly, and some come with a skip and a jump. The important thing is that they come. God is sovereign in His work and does not deal with all people in exactly the same way. Jesus healed at least three blind men during His earthly ministry, and He used a different method each time.

On a few occasions, the Lord Jesus used the shock ap-

---

[2]Paul Little, *How to Give Away Your Faith* (Downers Grove, Ill.: InterVarsity, 1966), p. 48.
[3]J. Oswald Sanders, *The Divine Art of Soul-Winning* (Chicago: Moody, n.d.), pp. 31-32.

proach. After listening to a compliment from Nicodemus (John 3:2), Jesus bluntly answered, "Except a man be born again, he cannot see the kingdom of God" (John 3:3). Such an approach must always be used with great care. Our Lord was never offensive or belligerent, but always sensitive to the needs of the individual.

Someone has warned, "If you want to gather honey, don't kick over the beehive." Be modest in every area, especially in your conversation. Avoid critical comments about other churches. You may be sold on your church, but remember to be modest. Seek to exalt Jesus Christ and honor the Word of God.

Remember to be kind and show love, even if your witness is rejected. Our responsibility is to share the gospel intelligently, sincerely, and sensitively. If we do that, we have fulfilled our responsibility. We all enjoy reaping, but we must remember that Jesus Christ is Lord of the harvest. He must give the increase.

The apostle Peter wrote, "Above all things have fervent charity [love] among yourselves: for charity shall cover the multitude of sins" (1 Peter 4:8).

It is interesting that Peter placed love above all things. He reminds us that God's love "shall cover a multitude of sins." Love really hides our shortcomings.

I have found that if my love is right, I do not have to worry about being offensive. Love really covers a multitude of sins. The apostle Paul warns each believer that apart from God's love, we are nothing (see 1 Corinthians 13:2). Here is a good question, "Is there anything less than nothing?"

Be at Ease

It seems to me that because of fear, the majority of Christians do not witness. It is much easier and safer not to become involved. Yet each believer *is* involved because of his position in Jesus Christ. We must overcome our fear and start sharing because God tells us to witness.

By nature, I happen to be shy. It was especially difficult for me to be at ease witnessing until I learned to claim God's strength and recognize my position in Jesus Christ. To begin with, I read and memorized verses like Romans 8:31, "If God be for us, who can be against us?" Always remember that almighty God is for us. At times you may be down on yourself, but God is for you. That is a life-changing thought, so take hold of it, and you will find strength to begin.

Often I have quoted and claimed 1 Corinthians 15:57, "Thanks be unto God who giveth us the victory through our Lord Jesus Christ." Victory is promised to each of us through Jesus Christ. Victory over fear, timidity, and even lack of training.

There is a popular philosophy based on the false foundation of the innate goodness and resourcefulness of man. Peddlers of hope encourage everyone to help himself to success, power, and wealth. But that concept is not biblical. The message of Scripture is not *help yourself*, but rather *yield yourself* (John 15:5). You can experience victory over fear in witnessing by yielding to Jesus Christ.

You see, in myself I cannot witness successfully, but through Christ, I can. Philippians 4:13 reads, "I can do all things through Christ which strengtheneth me." The key to overcoming the barriers of fear and timidity is to realize that Jesus Christ is working through us. I can't, but He can. I am not able, but God is able. When I look within, I become very discouraged. I see all kinds of faults and shortcomings, but in Christ all the obstacles are cut down to size. Christ is able! When I look without at the world, I am overwhelmed by human need. Yet once again in and through Jesus Christ, I can rise above the obstacles. For every need we have, there is a corresponding supply in Jesus Christ.

Why not write 1 John 4:4 on a card and carry it with you to remind you to live in the light of its truth: "Greater is he that is in you, than he that is in the world." The indwelling Holy Spirit is fully adequate to meet every obstacle. Allow Him to have complete authority, and you will be ready mentally to witness successfully.

PHYSICAL PREPARATION

There is an interesting verse in 1 Samuel 16:7, "The LORD said unto Samuel, Look not on his countenance, or on the height of his stature; because I have refused him: for the LORD seeth not as man seeth; for man looketh on the outward appearance, but the LORD looketh on the heart."

Two important facts given in this verse are that man looks at the outward appearance and that the Lord looks at the heart.

God is primarily interested in the inner man. The Lord looks upon the real you. If the heart is not right, nothing else can be right.

Man, on the other hand, can only see the outward appearance, and so his evaluation is based on external qualities. Consequently, when we witness, we must be concerned with our outward appearance.

Good grooming and outward appearance are important to successful witnessing. Unshined shoes and baggy pants detract from our witness. Poor color combinations, extreme styles, and immodest clothing can hurt our attempts to share the Good News. Take care that you dress in such a way as to support your witness rather than undermine it. Dress attractively, yet modestly. Flamboyant clothing can hinder just as much as a careless appearance. Neatness helps establish trust and acceptance. Guard against offensive breath or body odor. Ask a loved one or friend to check you out in these areas.

REMINDERS
- Clean hands and a pure heart are indispensable assets to witnessing.
- God loves people and so must we.

- Before we speak to people about God, it is important that we speak to God about people.
- The message of Scripture is not *help yourself*, but rather *yield yourself*.
- For every need you have, there is a corresponding supply in the power of Jesus Christ.
- If you want to gather honey, don't kick over the beehive.

QUESTIONS

1. Why is the assurance of salvation indispensable to witnessing?
2. Memorize Philippians 4:13 and tell how it applies to mental preparation.
3. Why should we be concerned about our outward appearance?
4. What do we mean by being tactful?
5. List five dos and don'ts of witnessing as suggested in this chapter.
6. Carefully write your testimony in 600 words and then commit it to memory.

Quite frankly, my urge to witness, to speak to others about Christ, has not always been constant. It varies. It comes and it goes. And almost without exception, my lack of loving concern is caused by some obstacle between the Lord and me. At such times, I seem unwilling to become involved, and I definitely lack interest. When this becomes apparent, I seek his face, humbly and honestly asking forgiveness. I then look into the faces around me with new interest. My heart and my eyes say to them, "God loves you . . . and . . . I care about you." When the time and place are right, I know someone whose heart has been "prepared" will be there, and Jesus Christ will walk right into the conversation. This usually happens when there is a river of out-going love from my heart.

Rosalind Rinker, in
You Can Witness with Confidence

3

WHY WITNESS?

David Ben Gurion, former prime minister of Israel, was asked what it would take to establish his new nation firmly. He laughed and replied, "All I need starts with the letter A—a lot of planes, a lot of guns, a lot of money, a lot of men."

We, too, could say that all a witness needs starts with the letter A—a lot of love, a lot of faith, a lot of wisdom, a lot of determination.

Witnessing, obviously, is not a thing that comes naturally to most people. Many people find it very difficult to share with other people the things of the Lord. And yet there are some very good reasons why we should witness. Let me suggest four reasons for witnessing.

BECAUSE OF THE REALITY
OF THE TRUTHS OF THE BIBLE

Some years ago Dr. Jonas Salk discovered the final phases of the polio vaccine. He had a means of freeing the world from the suffering and pain caused by the dread disease polio. Suppose he had decided to withhold that lifesaving vaccine. Such action would have been criminal.

In the same way, we as Christians have in the gospel truth that can free people from the power of sin. Can we sit idly by and watch people die in sin without giving them the good news that Christ died for them? Of course we cannot—if we really accept the truths of God's Word.

Do you believe the Lord Jesus when He says that who-ever is not a believer is condemned (John 3:18)? And do you believe Him when He describes hell, where "the fire is not quenched" (Mark 9:46)? And do you believe that Jesus is the only way to God (John 14:6)? If we really believe those things, nothing will be able to keep us from witnessing.

BECAUSE OF MY POSSESSION OF SALVATION

To enjoy salvation automatically makes me responsible. To have means to owe. Second Kings 7:3-9 presents the story of four starving lepers outside the gates of Samaria. Their situation was desperate. As lepers they were for-bidden to enter the city, yet if they did not get food, they would soon die. They decided to cast themselves upon the mercy of the Syrians. Upon entering the camp, they found it deserted. The Scripture reads, "For the Lord had made the host of the Syrians to hear a noise of chariots, and a noise of horses, even the noise of a great host. . . . Wherefore they arose and fled in the twilight. . . . And when these lepers came to the uttermost part of the camp, they went into one tent, and did eat and drink. . . . Then they said one to another, *We do not well: this day is a day of good tidings, and we hold our peace*" (2 Kings 7:6-9, emphasis added). Those lepers had a responsibility to share their newfound blessings with the masses of other hungry people.

That powerful idea applies to everyone who possesses salvation and for one reason or other fails to witness. It is essentially a sin to be silent. Our blessings make us re-sponsible.

The apostle Paul, writing to the church at Rome, re-minds us that we have a debt.

> I am debtor both to the Greeks, and to the Barbarians; both to the wise, and to the unwise. So, as much as in me is, I am ready to preach the gospel to you that are at Rome also. For I am not ashamed of the gospel of Christ: for it is the power of God unto salvation to every one that be-

28

lieveth; to the Jew first, and also to the Greek (Romans 1:14-16).

Contrary to the view of many people today, the world does not owe any of us a thing. But we as believers owe the world an intelligent, loving presentation of God's Good News.

The Old Testament prophet Ezekiel presents an answer to the question, "Why witness?" Listen to the Lord's words to him,

> When I say unto the wicked, O wicked man, thou shalt surely die; if thou dost not speak to warn the wicked from his way, that wicked man shall die in his iniquity; but his blood will I require at thine hand. Nevertheless, if thou warn the wicked of his way to turn from it; if he do not turn from his way, he shall die in his iniquity; but thou hast delivered thy soul (Ezekiel 33:8-9).

God is telling Ezekiel that he has the privilege and responsibility to warn people. Failure to sound the warning would result in his being held accountable. The same principle applies to Christians today.

The guilt of the priest and Levite in Luke 10 was that they saw the man on the Jericho road stripped, wounded, and half dead, and they passed by on the other side. Their sin was that they did nothing.

In the parable of the talents (Matthew 25:14-30), the worker with one talent was condemned because he did nothing with his possession. Our personal possession of God's great salvation makes us responsible. To do nothing is to sin.

BECAUSE OF THE GREAT COMMISSION

After the ascension of Jesus Christ, His disciples were anxious to know when the Kingdom of God would be established. Jesus told them, "It is not for you to know the times or the seasons, which the Father hath put in his own power" (Acts 1:7). After telling them what they were

29

not to know, He outlined exactly what they were to know. Jesus seemed to say, know this, "Ye shall receive power, after that the Holy Ghost is come upon you: and ye shall be witnesses unto me both in Jerusalem, and in all Judea, and in Samaria, and unto the uttermost part of the earth" (Acts 1:8). The great commission is so plain that no sincere believer in Jesus Christ can claim ignorance. Our Lord stated, "Ye shall be witnesses unto me."

William Carey read Matthew 28 and was burdened for a perishing, unbelieving world. He thought, *Does this commission of Jesus apply to me? Does God really want me to go as a missionary to share the good news?"* Carey decided to share his burden for witnessing with the local ministerium. The presiding pastor sternly rebuked young Carey and informed him that when God wanted to save the heathen, He would do it without his help. In spite of that rebuke, William Carey responded to the commission given by Jesus. He accepted his responsibility to share the Good News and became a missionary to India.

Just as God the Father sent His Son into this world, so God the Son sends each of us to communicate His love. This divine succession that we have brings an awesome responsibility. "As my Father hath sent me," said Jesus, "even so send I you" (John 20:21).

BECAUSE OF OUR POSITION AS AMBASSADORS
OF JESUS CHRIST

The apostle Paul was sensitive concerning his position before God. He said, "Now then we are ambassadors for Christ, as though God did beseech you by us: we pray you in Christ's stead, be ye reconciled to God" (2 Corinthians 5:20).

It is sobering to realize that God is making His appeal to the lost world through you and me. Charles B. Williams translates 2 Corinthians 5:20 powerfully, "So I am an envoy to represent Christ, because it is through me that God is making His appeal. As one representing Christ, I beg you, be ye reconciled to God."

With that awesome position, we are very much responsible. Each Christian is either a good ambassador of Christ or a poor one, but we cannot escape being ambassadors. In the light of this staggering truth, accept your position with great care.

Our responsibility to witness is plainly taught in the Bible, and God's provision is available. Of course, each of us feels inadequate. It is only as we lay hold of the strength and wisdom of God that we are able to witness successfully.

Let me list some biblical answers to the question "Why witness?"

1. Because we have *a debt* to the whole world (Romans 1:14).
2. Because *our knowledge* of the gospel makes us responsible (Ezekiel 33:8, 9).
3. Because *our blessing* demands that we share (2 Kings 7:6-9).
4. Because of the *great commission.* We have the word of reconciliation (2 Corinthians 5:19-21).
5. Because of *the love of Christ* (2 Corinthians 5:14).
6. Because of *the costly work of Christ* (2 Corinthians 5:15).
7. Because of *the terror of the Lord* (2 Corinthians 5:11).
8. Because of *the judgment of each believer* concerning our stewardship (2 Corinthians 5:10).
9. Because of *our position as ambassadors of Christ* (2 Corinthians 5:20).

During the reign of Oliver Cromwell, there was a shortage of currency in the British Empire. Representatives carefully searched the nation in hope of finding silver to meet the emergency. After one month, the committee returned with its findings. "We have searched the empire in vain seeking to find silver. To our dismay, we found none anywhere except in the cathedrals where the saints are carved from choice silver."

To this, Oliver Cromwell eloquently answered, "Let's melt down the saints and put them into circulation." Why not ask the Lord to melt you down for greater spiritual circulation.

REMINDERS

- All believers owe a debt simply because they possess God's salvation.
- To rattle off Bible verses mechanically with the hope of somehow discharging our spiritual responsibility is a farce.
- It is essentially a sin to be silent.
- The great commission is so plain that no sincere believer in Jesus Christ can claim ignorance.
- Each Christian is either a good ambassador for Jesus Christ or a poor one, but we cannot escape being ambassadors.

QUESTIONS

1. What is the implication of the phrase from Ezekiel 38:9, "but his blood will be required at thine hand"?
2. Why do we study the Bible in the light of 2 Timothy 2:15?
3. What was the sin of the priest and Levite in Luke chapter 10?
4. Explain how "the great commission" makes each believer responsible.
5. Memorize the following verses: Romans 1:14; Ezekiel 33:8-9; and 2 Corinthians 5:20.
6. List at least four reasons each believer should be a witness.

Non-Christians first need to detect the reality of genuine Christian experience in our lives. Then they will be attracted by our words about Jesus Christ and what it means to know Him personally. After I have spoken to a group, students often approach me with personal questions: "How does it work?" "How can I have the kind of life you've been talking about?" "Is there any hope for me?" It's always a privilege to sit down and explain how forgiveness, cleansing, and power can be individually ours in and through the Lord Jesus Christ.

Paul E. Little, in
How to Give Away Your Faith

4

HOW JESUS WITNESSED

A sports event has been described as an occasion where thousands of fans who desperately need exercise gather to watch the vigorous competition of a few athletes who desperately need a rest. Unfortunately, the spectator attitude has also moved into the church, causing the gospel to go unheard.

Jesus plainly taught that every true believer is a witness (Acts 1:8). The moment I received Jesus Christ as Saviour, my witness began. Remember, witnessing goes beyond what we say, to what we are, and what we do.

Dr. R. A. Torrey, the second president of Moody Bible Institute, said, "My one ambition in life is to win as many souls as I possibly can. It is the most worthwhile thing in life."

In talking with thousands of Christian students and church workers, I have discovered that there are common problems we all face. Most want to witness but just do not know *how to start*. If that is your problem, I believe this chapter will help you. In the Bible, Jesus is called the true and faithful witness. John 4 shows step by step how Jesus witnessed. Our Lord was the greatest witness who ever lived. As the *incomparable witness* He illustrates specifically what to do in witnessing.

A DIVINE COMPULSION

In John 4 we find Jesus and His disciples traveling from Judea to Galilee. Contrary to the usual custom, they

35

traveled through the land of Samaria. John mentions that interesting fact, saying that Jesus "must needs go through Samaria" (John 4:4). But why? There certainly were other roads on which they could have traveled. In fact, an orthodox Jew would take the long road across the Jordan River through Peraea and then back into Galilee just so he would not have to travel through Samaria. The orthodox Jew looked with disdain on all Samaritans because they were a mixed race of people.

Why then did Jesus travel through Samaria? He didn't go that way simply because it was geographically closer. That would not have been in keeping with the social customs of the day. No, Jesus made a special point of journeying through Samaria for the sole purpose of witnessing to the Samaritan woman.

The word "must" in John 4:4 implies logical necessity. "He must needs go through Samaria." It is a term we would use to say, "a triangle must have three sides." It is used here to convey God's intention to reach this woman. The word "must" sparkles with the light of divine purpose. And divine compulsion is an important key to all successful witnessing. Each witness should know and feel something of the concern of God. There must be that inner divine compulsion to share the good news.

It is interesting to notice that Jesus did not begin witnessing by asking this woman a tricky theological question. Jesus began by trying to meet her spiritual need. Simply and kindly, He led her step by step to see her condition. We must do the same.

PEOPLE ARE THIRSTY

What do we know about this woman? We know that she was thirsty. John tells us it was "about the sixth hour" (John 4:6), or just about noontime. Noontime is hot in Samaria, and this woman had come to draw fresh drinking water from the well on the outskirts of the city of Sychar.

In John 3, we saw Jesus talking with a man—
Nicodemus, the leader of the Jews. Here in this chapter,
He witnesses to a woman. What a contrast in those two
people! Nicodemus was a Jew, and this woman was a
Samaritan. He was a brilliant scholar; she was probably of
average intelligence. Nicodemus was a moral, respected
leader of high social position. The woman at the well was
immoral and living with a man who was not her husband.
Nicodemus had gone to Jesus, but Jesus went to the
woman.

Yet underneath all their external differences, both of
these people were thirsty and in need of God's salvation.
In reality, all mankind is on a never ending search, seeking answers to the gigantic questions it faces. I saw a sign
on a car not long ago that said, "Don't follow me, I'm
lost." That describes the condition of the vast majority of
people.

Carl Jung, the noted psychologist, has said, "Man is an
enigma to himself." A sense of despair and lostness
characterizes many. Mankind has an inner thirst to be
right with God. A good question is, Are we aware of the
great spiritual thirst around us? Are we concerned with
the fact that the people with whom we work or go to
school are helpless apart from Jesus Christ?

PEOPLE ARE RELIGIOUS

Not only do we know that this woman was thirsty, but
we also know that she was, in a certain sense, a religious
person. Pascal, the French mathematician and philoso-
pher, said, "There is a God-shaped vacuum in every
heart." And of course, only God can fill that. But people
try to fill it with religion. Whether we acknowledge it or
not, most people are religious. This woman knew all
about the religious heritage of the Jews (verse 12). And
verse 25 tells us that she was even expecting the Messiah
to come. Perhaps she secretly longed for personal deliverance from her enslaving lusts.

She also was aware of the religious controversy that raged in that day. In fact, verse 20 shows that she was ready to debate the validity of Mt. Gerizim over Jerusalem as the correct place to worship. She no doubt had a significant awareness of the Old Testament and its teachings.

But despite her religious knowledge, she was empty-hearted. It is encouraging to know that no matter who we are, no matter what the nature of our need, Jesus is adequate to meet those needs. Christ is the answer to every situation in life! He is fully able to quench that deep thirst within. Jesus knew all about this woman just as He knows all about each one of us. Everything is known to Him.

FOUR PRINCIPLES OF WITNESSING USED BY JESUS

Jesus Asked a Favor

Our Lord did not start witnessing to the woman by telling her that she was a prostitute. The kindness of Jesus was demonstrated in a sensitive approach to this woman. "Give me to drink," He asked (verse 7). He knew that one of the best ways to win someone's confidence is to ask a simple favor. Kindness often penetrates the most difficult personality. He did not say, "Lady, do you know who I am?" He began at a point of common interest—their mutual need for water. By a series of steps Jesus got to her heart.

The first rule in successful witnessing is to gain the interest and attention of those to whom we witness. I have watched some people plunge right in, rattling off verses and not even taking the time to introduce themselves, let alone conduct a normal conversation. Our approach is sometimes crude, and we fail because we have not taken the effort and care to establish a common, thoughtful, courteous point of interest. How did Jesus begin? He began by kindly asking a simple favor.

To ask a favor of someone is often a form of a compliment. It indicates that the other person possesses something that you desire or admire.

Jesus Refused to Argue

When Jesus asked for water, the woman responded, "How is it that thou, being a Jew, askest drink of me, which am a woman of Samaria?" (verse 9). She immediately raised the question of racial prejudice. "Why are you talking with me when you should hate me?" she seemed to say.

But Jesus refused to be drawn into an argument. He knew that attitudes of racial discrimination were wrong, but He did not debate with the woman. Rather, Jesus demonstrated in a practical way that He sincerely cared.

At times, in our attempts to witness for Christ, we get caught up in heated arguments that usually cause more harm than good. Remember the little couplet "A man convinced against his will/Is of the same opinion still." It is possible to win the argument and lose the person. The apostle James reminds Christians to "be swift to hear, slow to speak, slow to wrath" (James 1:19). Nothing profitable is accomplished when we try to force men and women to accept Christ. Jesus did not argue. Contend for the faith, but don't be contentious.

Jesus Aroused Her Interest

John 4:10 says, "Jesus answered and said unto her, If thou knewest the gift of God, and who it is that saith to thee, Give me to drink; thou wouldest have asked of him, and he would have given thee living water." He seemed to say somewhat teasingly, "I know something you don't know." The fact that He knew something she did not know aroused her curiosity.

That certainly does not mean that we are supposed to do strange things. At times some people will think we are odd enough, but that does not give us the excuse to be ridiculous in our behavior or methods. The late Paul Little wrote, "Oddballism may momentarily arouse curiosity about us, but it tends to discourage true interest in the gospel."

I have found that a helpful way to arouse interest is simply to ask a person, "By the way, are you interested in spiritual things?" If he says yes, I proceed by sharing what Jesus Christ means to me. If he says no, I ask, "What do you think it means to be a Christian?" Often those two questions will open the door to a fruitful opportunity to witness. Jesus aroused the interest and curiosity of the Samaritan woman.

Jesus Awakened Her Conscience

To be effective witnesses we must probe the area of need. Jesus got to the heart of the matter. In verse 16, He said to the woman, "Go, call thy husband, and come hither." Outwardly that seemed like a simple and innocent request. But actually it dug deep into her past life. She answered, "I have no husband. Jesus said unto her, Thou hast well said, I have no husband: for thou hast had five husbands; and he whom thou now hast is not thy husband: in that saidst thou truly. The woman saith unto him, Sir, I perceive that thou art a prophet" (John 4:17-19).

What the woman really was saying was, "You are right, I am a sinner and I need help. I am thirsty." Jesus awakened her conscience. He hit upon her point of weakness, and she saw herself for what she really was—a sinner needing salvation.

It is interesting and exciting to see the change in this woman's thinking as her conversation with Jesus developed. In verse 9 she called Him a Jew, just a traveler. In verse 12, she suggested that possibly He might be greater than Jacob. In verse 19, she called Him a prophet, and in verse 29 she declared Him to be the Messiah.

What a beautiful and powerful example of soul-winning this is. This woman's conversation with Jesus was so meaningful, so life-changing, that she forgot her water pots and hurried off to the city to tell her friends about Jesus. She was changed from a harlot to a herald of the gospel.

One of the many lessons in John 4 is the important lesson of learning the true needs of those to whom we witness. If we sincerely care for others, they will sense our love and give us a hearing.

The woman of Samaria met Jesus and He met her needs. She came to the well seeking water to quench her physical thirst and she went away with the water of eternal life, never to thirst again.

This woman's life was so dramatically transformed that her friends could not wait to see for themselves what had happened to her. "And many of the Samaritans of that city believed on him for the saying of the woman, which testified, He told me all that ever I did" (John 4:39). They also came to Jesus and believed and experienced salvation. No witness can do better than copy Jesus.

REMINDERS

- Witnessing goes beyond what we say, to what we really are and what we do.
- "There is a God-shaped vacuum in every heart."
                                        Blaise Pascal
- The first rule in successful witnessing is to gain the interest and attention of those to whom we witness.
- "A man convinced against his will is of the same opinion still."
- "Oddballism may momentarily arouse curiosity about us, but it tends to discourage true interest in the gospel" (Paul Little).

QUESTIONS

1. Why did Jesus travel through Samaria?
2. How would you go about proving that all mankind possesses an inner thirst?
3. Why should one seek to avoid an argument in witnessing?
4. Trace the dramatic change in the Samaritan woman's thinking as Jesus spoke to her.

5. What proof is there that the woman of Samaria was changed by the witness of Jesus?
6. List the four principles Jesus used in witnessing in John chapter 4.

No man at one and the same time can show that he himself is clever—and that Jesus Christ is mighty to save.

James Denney

The real question is not, "Is this the best time for a personal word for Christ?" but it is "Am I willing to improve this time for Christ, and for a precious soul, whether it is the best time or not?" If the Christian waits until the sinner gives sign of a desire for help, or until the Christian thinks that a loving word to the sinner will be most timely, he is not likely to begin at all. The only safe rule for his guidance—if indeed a Christian needs a specific rule as a guide—is to speak lovingly of Christ and of Christ's love for the individual whenever one has an opportunity of choosing his subject of conversation in an interview with an individual who may be in special need, yet who has given no special indication of it.

Henry Clay Trumbull, in
Individual Work for Individuals

5

HOW PHILIP, A LAYMAN, WITNESSED

Someone has said that the problem with many Christians is that we suffer from spiritual lockjaw. Unfortunately, that is true. This spiritual sickness is widespread and found among people of all ages. There are literally thousands of Christians who have never told one other person about who Jesus is and what He has done for them.

Perhaps many of those Christians fear failure or rejection. The example of Philip shows us guidelines about how to witness, without failure or unnecessary rejection. We would do well to follow his example.

The account of Philip's witness is found in Acts 8:26-40. In that passage we find six characteristics of the successful witness.

THE SUCCESSFUL WITNESS MUST BE OBEDIENT TO THE VOICE OF GOD

Philip was probably a Greek-speaking Jew, a deacon in the early church. He was greatly concerned about reaching the people beyond the borders of Judea, and he was one of the first to go outside the circle of Judaism to share the Good News. The apostles in the Jerusalem church decided to give themselves to the ministry of prayer and the Word (Acts 6:4), as Philip, the deacon, felt compelled to share the gospel with the people in nearby Samaria.

The response to his sharing was so overwhelming that "the people with one accord gave heed unto those things which Philip spake" (Acts 8:6). "And there was great joy in that city" (verse 8). Philip enjoyed the kind of spiritual results that many of us dream about.

But at the very peak of Philip's witnessing, the Lord told him to leave the city, the crowds, and the results and go down to Gaza, a desert place some 80 miles away. Verse 26 reads, "And the angel of the Lord spake unto Philip, saying, Arise, and go toward the south, unto the way that goeth down from Jerusalem unto Gaza, which is desert." Common sense would seem to tell him to stay in Samaria, where he was having success, but the voice of God was clear. The Lord literally led Philip from the crowded city to the barren desert, from the masses of people to a single soul. Here is a lesson each of us must learn—God's ways are not always our ways. Had Philip made a list of the reasons for staying or for going, he would probably have stayed. It is necessary that we always obey the voice of God.

Philip's response to the Lord's command was immediate. Verse 27 reads, "And he arose and went." He had absolute trust in God that His orders were right. He did not argue, debate, discuss, or delay, "he arose and went." May we, too, be quick to obey the voice of God.

During a particular period in World War II, the North African campaign was seriously bogged down because a number of enlisted men had lost confidence in their officers. The resulting poor morale and poor fighting nearly proved to be disastrous.

It can be exactly that way with us. We dare not hesitate to move when God speaks. Had Philip relied on what might have seemed like common sense, had he continued his witness where he had been so successful, he would have stayed in the city of Samaria. But God had other plans for him. The first, second, and last rule in witnessing is obedience to the will and voice of God.

Philip's response reminds me of Abraham. God spoke to Abraham and said, "Take now thy son, thine only son

Isaac, whom thou lovest, and get thee into the land of Moriah; and offer him there for a burnt offering" (Genesis 22:3). The command of the Lord seemed contrary to all God had promised. Isaac was the miracle child. Through Isaac, all the promises of God would be realized. Yet in spite of all that, Abraham did not hesitate. He rose up early and obeyed God.

Just so, as we take the first step in faith, the other steps will come more easily. Always remember that we walk by faith and not by sight. The best way to see far ahead in the will of God is to go as far ahead as you can see. Faithfulness today will automatically prepare you for what God has tomorrow.

THE SUCCESSFUL WITNESS MUST RECOGNIZE THAT THE GOSPEL IS FOR ALL MEN

As Philip traveled toward Gaza, he came upon a caravan of soldiers and merchants, and in the center, the treasurer of Ethiopia. Here was the man to whom Philip had been sent to share the gospel. Who was this person to whom God sent Philip?

He Was Probably a Gentile

We are told that the eunuch had just been to Jerusalem to worship. Some have suggested that he may have been a Jew who had reached a high place in the government of Ethiopia. Joseph, who became a ruler in Egypt, and Daniel, who reached a high position in Babylon, are examples of Jews who prospered in foreign lands. However, most Bible students believe that this man was a Gentile who had been converted to Judaism.

He Was Probably a Black Man

Always remember that the inclusive gospel cannot be shared by exclusive people. To label people as worthy or unworthy, as acceptable or unacceptable, is inconsistent with the grace of God. To do so is thoroughly anti-scriptural and anti-Christian (James 2:5-9). Every person, regardless of outward differences, is made in the image of God and loved by God. Since the eunuch was an Ethiopian, he probably was a black man.

In Jesus Christ there is neither Jew nor Greek, bond nor free, male nor female. The Body of Christ includes all races. The gospel is for every race. We cannot afford to discriminate in our witnessing.

He Was a Statesman

He was involved in the government of a great country. He was a man of influence. He had great authority. Actually he was in charge of the government's money and served as secretary of the treasury.

The gospel is not only for all races but for all levels of humanity—the up and out as well as the down and out.

He Was Religious

The Scriptures tell us that he "had come to Jerusalem for to worship" (Acts 8:27). This man recognized that he possessed a soul, and he went to great lengths to meet his spiritual needs. He was really a seeker of truth, and Philip found him reading the Old Testament prophecy of Isaiah.

No matter who we are, no matter where we have come from, the good news of the gospel is for all. God is no respecter of persons. The great commission of our Lord was, "Go ye into all the world, and preach the gospel to every creature" (Mark 16:15). Philip recognized this and we must too.

THE SUCCESSFUL WITNESS MUST SHARE
HIS FAITH WITH ENTHUSIASM

Philip had an inner fire. The Bible says he ran to meet the eunuch (Acts 8:30). Philip was a Spirit-led and Spirit-filled man. He was in a hurry to do the will of God. He was excited.

Most of us need some heavenly enthusiasm. Abraham Lincoln said, "I like to see a man preach like he is fighting bees." The word *enthusiasm* really means to be influenced or inspired by God. If any people ought to radiate enthusiasm and joy, we should.

We read that the apostolic church was "Praising God, and having favour with all the people" (Acts 2:47). Their unanimous acceptance was related to their spirit of praise. There is a charisma in praise. "Praise is comely for the upright" (Psalm 33:1).

A sad, half-hearted, reluctant Christian is an enigma. But when the joy of the Lord is our strength, we must say with Peter, "We cannot but speak" what we know and believe. Ask the Lord to make you a winsome witness, and I guarantee you that you will win some. Enthusiasm isn't everything but it is important.

THE SUCCESSFUL WITNESS MUST ESTABLISH A POINT OF CONTACT

Notice the way Philip began his witness to this Ethiopian eunuch. Because the man was reading the Scriptures, Philip took a very direct approach. He asked, "Understandest thou what thou readest?" (Acts 8:30). To get the full impact of the directness of this question, try to imagine someone approaching the Secretary of the Treasury of the United States and asking, "Do you understand what you are reading?"

Jesus occasionally used the blunt approach, and so did Paul. Philip probably startled the Ethiopian, but apparently the Ethiopian recognized that Philip was from God. When we are truly led by the Spirit of God and sensitive to the needs of people, God will care for the response. I'm afraid that too many of us are so tactful that we don't even make contact. Too often we are more concerned about what people think than about what God thinks. Tact is important. We are to be as "wise as serpents, and harmless as doves" (Matthew 10:16). Strive for the balance of a tough mind and a tender heart.

The Ethiopian answered, "How can I [understand] except some man should guide me?" (Acts 8:31). The Ethiopian needed help, and Philip was ready to guide him. It is thrilling to realize that God permits us to guide people into an understanding of His Word.

THE SUCCESSFUL WITNESS
MUST KNOW THE SCRIPTURES

The Bible account says, "Then Philip opened his mouth, and began at the same Scripture, and preached unto him Jesus" (Acts 8:35). As God's witnesses, we must be ready to open our mouths and share what the Bible teaches. An understanding of what it teaches is necessary. We are told to divide the word of truth rightly. Peter tells Christians to "be ready always to give an answer to every man that asketh you a reason of the hope that is in you" (1 Peter 3:15). Do you know how to lead a person to Christ? Can you share the meaning of the Scriptures with another?

Notice how God worked to pinpoint the Ethiopian's spiritual need. The man was reading from Isaiah 53. He had been to Jerusalem and was returning home, evidently spiritually empty. He was searching that great Messianic passage in Isaiah, but he could not understand it.

Had Philip not responded to the Holy Spirit as he did, this man would have returned home in his ignorance. He would not have known the salvation he found in Jesus Christ. Philip immediately entered into the Ethiopian's experience at the point of his need. He read the passage, "He was led as a sheep to the slaughter." And to answer the question, "To whom does this refer?" Philip "began at the same scripture, and preached unto him Jesus" (Acts 8:35). Is your knowledge of Scripture adequate so that you can use it to minister to people at their point of greatest need?

I am sure that many other questions were asked and answered in their exchange. Evidently Philip took this man through the entire gospel story. I believe he told him of Jesus' birth, His life, His teaching, His suffering, and His death for all. He must have told him of the resurrection and the new life offered in Jesus Christ, of the great

50

commission, and of the importance of confessing Christ openly. Soon the Ethiopian was ready to make a life-changing decision.

THE SUCCESSFUL WITNESS MUST SEEK A DECISION

As they approached a body of water, the Ethiopian asked, "Here is water; what doth hinder me to be baptized?" (Acts 8:36). How did he know about being baptized? Evidently Philip had presented the gospel so completely and convincingly that the Ethiopian was prepared to believe and be baptized. Philip answered, "If thou believest . . . thou mayest. And he answered and said, I believe that Jesus Christ is the Son of God" (Acts 8:37). Upon hearing his confession, Philip baptized him.

Philip had witnessed effectively. The Ethiopian was changed by the power of the gospel. No doubt a new light was on his face and a new thrill in his spirit. He was mastered by a new love—the love of Jesus Christ. Philip, the layman, had successfully witnessed concerning Jesus Christ, and a soul had been converted.

Philip's experience in witnessing gives us six important principles to remember and practice:
1. Be obedient to the voice of God.
2. Recognize that the gospel is for all men.
3. Share the gospel with enthusiasm.
4. Establish a point of contact and open your mouth.
5. Know the Scriptures.
6. Seek for a decision.
Philip was in a hurry to obey the Lord.

REMINDERS

- First, second, last, and always, the witness must be obedient to the voice of God.
- Faithfulness today will automatically prepare you for what God has for you tomorrow.
- Always remember that the inclusive gospel cannot be shared by exclusive people.

- Abraham Lincoln said, "I like to see a man preach like he is fighting bees."
- Too many of us are so tactful that we don't even make contact.

QUESTIONS

1. Does the will of God always correspond with what we might consider common sense? Illustrate this in the experience of Philip in Acts, chapter 8.
2. List four thoughts that provide background concerning the Ethiopian.
3. What does the word "enthusiasm" mean? How did Philip show his enthusiasm? How can we?
4. In what way was Philip's approach in witnessing blunt?
5. List six characteristics of the successful witness.

There are at least two ways of serving a meal. I could come to a table that is beautifully spread, with Texas-size T-bone steaks, mashed potatoes, parsley peas, iced tea with a slice of lemon, molded Jello salad garnished with cheddar cheese, and cherry pie piled high with whipped cream. That is, I could if I were not dieting.

A second kind of meal can consist of one huge bowl of food served on a bare table. Suppose I ask my wife, "What in the world is this?"

"I'm sorry, honey," she says, "I just didn't have time to prepare the meal in the usual way, so I took the steak, the peas, the mashed potatoes, the salad, and the cherry pie, and I put them all together with the iced tea. It's the best I could do."

The meals are equally nourishing, but not equally appetizing. Our witnessing is like those two meals in some ways.

You may not be serving up verbal hash in your witnessing, but on the other hand you may not be offering a delectable spread, either.

Howard G. Hendricks, in
Say It with Love

How then does one actually receive Jesus Christ? In Revelation 3:20 Jesus Christ compares our lives to a house and says, "Behold I stand at the door and knock. If any man hears my voice and opens the door, I will come in to him and eat with him and he with me." Showing him this verse, I often ask an interested student, "Suppose someone came to the door of your room and knocked. How would you get the person inside?" The student thinks for a moment and then says, "Why I'd open the door." I say, "Exactly. And then what would you do?" Invariably they respond, "I'd invite the person in." Usually a flash of insight crosses their face as they realize that this is exactly how one becomes a Christian. The Lord Jesus Christ is knocking at the door of our lives. He will not gate-crash or force His way in but will come in at our invitation. This invitation can be given Him simply in our own words in prayer. And when we receive Him, He promises to come in and be with us for eternity.

Paul E. Little, in
How to Give Away Your Faith

6

PRESENTING THE GOSPEL

No one calls for a doctor until he realizes he is sick. Just so, it is helpful for people to understand something of the nature and results of sin before they desire and fully appreciate the good news of salvation. But what is the best way to introduce the subject?

There is no perfect way for everyone. I like to begin with a simple, direct question like, "What do you think of Jesus Christ?" or "Are you interested in spiritual things?" Regardless of the answer given, those questions make it possible to get to the heart of the gospel.

I sometimes ask, "What will Jesus Christ do with you?"; "How good are you in God's sight?"; "Do you know what I mean when I speak about a spiritual birthday?"; or, "Is God satisfied with your religion?"

Sometimes I begin by asking, "May I tell you how I know for sure that I'm going to heaven?" or, "Why should God take you to heaven?" Other times I will open the conversation with an attractive piece of literature or a tract. There are many good ways to open the conversation. The important thing in all our witnessing is to be thoughtful of the rights of others and sensitive to the guidance of the Holy Spirit of God.

In presenting the gospel, I include *five areas*.

SHOW THEM THEIR NEED OF SALVATION

The Bible plainly states that every person has a spiritual need. I like to open my Bible and read directly from the Scriptures. Robert Murray McCheyne said, "It is not our comment on the Word that saves, but the Word itself." Often I will ask the one to whom I'm witnessing to read the verse for himself. For example, Romans 3:23 states, "For all have sinned and come short of the glory of God."

I have the person read that verse, and then I explain that some people have apparently sinned less than others, but the fact is—*all* have sinned. All of us have fallen short of what God requires. We have failed in thought, word, and deed. Each one of us has a deep spiritual need and none of us can meet that need by his own efforts.

Often I turn to the Old Testament and refer to Isaiah 53:6, "All we like sheep have gone astray; we have turned every one to his own way; and the LORD hath laid on him the iniquity of us all."

The first part of that verse, "All we like sheep have gone astray," states clearly our need. The second part of the verse, "the LORD hath laid on him the iniquity of us all," tells of God's provision for our need.

Occasionally I will follow the reading of this verse with a number of questions. For example, "My friend, have you gone astray from God? Have you turned to your own way? If so, according to this verse what is your condition?" I like to comment on the lostness of all men.

Then I might ask, "If the Lord has laid your iniquity on Christ, is it on you any longer?" Simple questions like that help nail down the truths of man's need as well as God's provision.

SHOW THEM THEY CANNOT SAVE THEMSELVES

Probably the greatest error that exists today is the belief that salvation is the result of personal effort. That is, that we can gain salvation by doing good things. I like to turn to the following passages, which tell us plainly that no one can save himself.

"Not by works of righteousness which we have done, but according to his mercy he saved us" (Titus 3:5).

"By the works of the law shall no flesh be justified" (Galatians 2:16).

56

"For whosoever shall keep the whole law, and yet offend in one point, he is guilty of all" (James 2:10).

"There is a way which seemeth right unto a man, but the end thereof are the ways of death" (Proverbs 14:12).

Thousands imagine themselves Christian because they seek to keep the golden rule or because they live decent, moral lives. Some rely upon their religious activity or church membership. In direct contrast, the apostle John says that salvation does not come through "the will of the flesh" (John 1:13).

The Bible message is plain on the subject and easy to understand. "For by grace are ye saved through faith; and that not of yourselves: it is the gift of God: not of works, lest any man should boast" (Ephesians 2:8,9).

Salvation is not *something you do* but *Someone you receive*. Salvation is Jesus Christ. It would be easier to tunnel through the mountains with teaspoons than to get to heaven by one's personal effort, character, or morality. Salvation is an offer, not a demand. It is not based on what I do, but on what Jesus Christ has done.

We do not become Christians by climbing the ladder of good works, rung by rung. Jesus Christ came by way of Bethlehem's manger and Calvary's cross to meet us where we are. No one can ever save himself.

SHOW THEM GOD'S PROVISION
FOR THEIR SALVATION

The good news of the gospel is that Almighty God intervened in history to provide salvation for sinful people like you and me. Paul announces it in Romans 5:8, "But God commendeth his love toward us, in that, while we were yet sinners, Christ died for us."

God's provision for our sin is seen clearly in the most familiar verse of Scripture. "For God so loved the world that he gave his only begotten Son, that whosoever believeth in him should not perish, but have everlasting life" (John 3:16). Years ago I discovered the importance of asking simple questions. After reading John 3:16, I like to ask, "Who is God's Son? What did God's Son accomplish on the cross for you? What does 'whosoever' mean? If you believe in God's Son, what will you receive?" All the conversation is directed toward presenting Jesus Christ as God's *provision* for *man's need.* Jesus emphatically stated, "I am the way, the truth, and the life; no man cometh unto the Father but by me" (John 14:6).

There are basically two important elements in conversion. They are *repentance* and *faith.* Explain the concepts to the person you are dealing with.

What is repentance? It is turning away from whatever is displeasing to God. It is to turn from our way to God's way. It involves a change of heart, attitude, and mind, and it results in a change of conduct.

What is faith? It is believing. It is receiving. It is not mere mental assent to a fact, rather it is trust in a Person. It is trusting in Jesus Christ alone for salvation and forgiveness of sin.

I ask the person to read John 3:36, and show him the importance of trusting Christ. "He that believeth on the Son hath everlasting life: and he that believeth not the Son shall not see life; but the wrath of God abideth on him" (John 3:36). At this point I usually ask, "Would you like to receive Jesus Christ as your personal Saviour?" Then I like to lead in a simple prayer of preparation.

"Heavenly Father, may this be the moment of salvation for Bill. The best he knows how, may he repent of his sins and wholly place his trust in Jesus Christ who died for him."

While our heads are bowed, I suggest that he pray the following prayer out loud after me, phrase by phrase.

"Lord Jesus, I invite You into my life right now. I confess that I am a sinner. I have been trusting in myself and my own efforts. But now I place my full trust in Jesus Christ alone. I believe You died on the cross for me. I accept You right now as my personal Saviour. Help me to turn from my sins and follow You. Thank You for receiving me into Your eternal family. Amen."

SHOW THEM HOW TO HAVE THE ASSURANCE
OF SALVATION

In 2 Corinthians 13:5, Paul encourages believers. "Examine yourselves, whether ye be in the faith." In 2 Peter 1:10, we are told, "Give diligence to make your calling and election sure." In other words, assurance is possible and even expected. The assurance of salvation is one of God's beautiful gifts to each believer. How can we know we are saved?

We Can Know by the Word of God

We begin with the Bible. Assurance of salvation is based upon acceptance of the Bible as the Word of God. As we apply the promises of Scripture to our lives, doubt leaves.

The apostle John knew the difficulties of doubt. John wrote, "These things have I written unto you that believe on the name of the Son of God; that ye may know that ye have eternal life, and that ye may believe on the name of the Son of God" (1 John 5:13). That verse should be memorized. The purpose is that "ye may know that ye have eternal life." The word *know* means "to recognize the quality of." The apostle John wrote these verses so that each believer might consciously recognize his position in Christ. This is not an opinion or a matter of inference, but a revelation from God.

We Can Know by the Witness Within

Assurance of salvation is possible by the witness of the Holy Spirit. At conversion, you became the dwelling place of the Holy Spirit. This heavenly Guest wants complete lordship in your life. Yielding to the indwelling Holy Spirit brings a definite sense of assurance of salvation.

Many, through carelessness and lack of knowledge,

59

grieve the Holy Spirit and know little or nothing of the witness within. Paul said, "Ye have received the Spirit of adoption, whereby we cry, Abba, Father" (Romans 8:15) or literally, "My own dear Father." That cry is born of the Holy Spirit.

SHOW THEM THAT JESUS CHRIST WILL ENABLE THEM TO OVERCOME TEMPTATION

"If any man be in Christ, he is a new creature: old things are passed away; behold, all things are become new" (2 Corinthians 5:17). "There hath no temptation taken you but such as is common to man: but God is faithful, who will not suffer you to be tempted above that ye are able; but will with the temptation also make a way to escape" (1 Corinthians 10:13).

How can we overcome temptation?

First, to the believer, the child of God, is given the privilege of prayer in overcoming temptation. James says, "If any [man] lack wisdom, let him ask of God, that giveth to all men [generously]" (James 1:5).

Do you need help in overcoming your weakness? Ask God! Do you need deliverance from the power and temptation of sin? Ask God! He alone is able to deliver you. Often I have cried out, "Lord, help me," and God's deliverance was given. D. L. Moody said, "When Christians find themselves exposed to temptation, they should pray to God to uphold them, and when they are tempted they should not be discouraged. It is not a sin to be tempted; the sin is to fall into temptation."

Second, apply the Word of God. Jesus put Satan to flight by quoting Scripture, and we also must fortify ourselves with the Word of God.

Third, submit to the indwelling Holy Spirit. To the child of God who is directed by the Holy Spirit, temptation may come, but it will not be able to destroy him. For God has promised, "Greater is he that is in you, than he that is in the world" (1 John 4:4).

In your hour of trial, remember that God is faithful. He

knows your capacity. He will give you all the strength you need to overcome temptation, or He will make a way of deliverance for you.

ADDITIONAL HELPS

Some organizations have prepared booklets and tracts to aid you in presenting the gospel. For nearly a century the Moody Bible Institute has published the little booklet, 4 *Things God Wants You to Know*. It contains appropriate Scripture verses about the way of salvation. Millions of copies have been effectively used around the world.

Recently the Moody Bible Institute has prepared an attractive booklet based on the international road signs and entitled 5 *Signs to a New Life*. Thousands have found it very helpful in presenting the way of salvation.

Here is a photographed copy of each page.

There is also the popular *Four Spiritual Laws* produced by Campus Crusade that many have used with much success.

My advice is to start where you are with what you know and present the gospel.

REMINDERS

- The good news of the gospel is that Almighty God intervened in history to provide salvation for sinful people like you and me.
- Yielding to the indwelling Holy Spirit brings definite assurance of salvation.
- Salvation is an offer, not a demand.
- Jesus put Satan to flight by quoting Scripture, and we also must fortify ourselves with the Word of God.
- "When Christians find themselves exposed to temptation, they should pray to God to uphold them, and when they are tempted, they should not be discouraged. It is not a sin to be tempted; the sin is to fall into temptation" (D. L. Moody).

5 Signs to a New Life

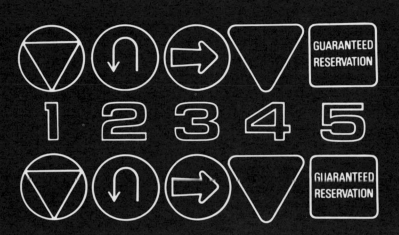

2

As signs along the highway help you reach your destination . . .

So there are signs to guide you safely through this life. Because *God loves and cares for you,* He places these signs in your path to lead you into an unending fellowship with Himself.

3

SIGN 1

Stop!

Recognize that, *if* you are proceeding under your own power, you are going in the wrong direction, away from God's help.

The Bible says:

"For all have sinned, and come short of the glory of God." ROMANS 3:23

"All we like sheep have gone astray; we have turned every one to his own way; and the Lord hath laid on him the iniquity of us all." ISAIAH 53:6

We cannot change ourselves or even change our ways without God's help.

5

Make a full turn . . .

Recognize your sinfulness and guilt before God and acknowledge that you are as helpless as He said.

Turn away from your sin and turn to Jesus Christ. This is called repentance.

6

ABUNDANT
LIFE-CHRIST

GODLESS
ETERNITY

"For the wages of sin is death; but the gift of God is eternal life through Jesus Christ our Lord." ROMANS 6:23

"Repent ye therefore, and be converted, that your sins may be blotted out..." ACTS 3:19

7

SIGN

3

Follow the ONE WAY that Jesus has mapped out in the Bible.

This one way brings you the forgiveness, peace, strength, understanding and love that Jesus has promised to all who trust Him for this new life.

8

Jesus says this about His ONE WAY:

"Jesus saith unto him, I am the way, the truth, and the life: no man cometh unto the Father, but by Me."
JOHN 14:6

"Peace I leave with you, My peace I give unto you: not as the world giveth, give I unto you. Let not your heart be troubled, neither let it be afraid." JOHN 14:27

"Come unto Me, all ye that labour and are heavy laden, and I will give you rest." MATTHEW 11:28

9

SIGN
4

Yield to God's Son, Jesus Christ.

He alone is able to provide forgiveness for your sin against God His Father, and to bring you into a personal relationship with Him. Christ's death on the cross is God's provision for our sins.

10

Jesus says:

"But God commendeth His love toward us, in that, while we were yet sinners, Christ died for us."   ROMANS 5:8

"For God so loved the world, that He gave His only begotten Son, that whosoever believeth in Him should not perish, but have everlasting life."   JOHN 3:16

He Rose from the Dead

"Christ died for our sins...He was buried...He rose again the third day according to the Scriptures."   I CORINTHIANS 15:3,4

WOULD YOU LIKE THIS NEW LIFE THAT GOD OFFERS?

11

If you want Jesus to give you a new life, ask Him for it in your own words . . . or you may want to use the following prayer.

Dear Jesus,

I see now that all my life I have been passing many "wrong direction" signs. I want you to turn me around, to take me out of my own way and put me in Yours.

I know that You are the only One who can do this. I am sorry for everything I have done that has displeased You and Your Father.

Please forgive me of my sins right now. Take me into Your spiritual family and give me eternal life.

From now on, direct my life completely—until I go to be with You in Heaven.

NAME _____ DATE _____

12

SIGN
5

If you prayed that prayer you can now ...Look forward to a GUARANTEED RESERVATION in heaven!

GUARANTEED RESERVATION

". . . Believe on the Lord Jesus Christ, and thou shalt be saved . . ."   ACTS 16:31

"In My Father's house are many mansions: if it were not so, I would have told you. I go to prepare a place for you."   JOHN 14:2

13

Jesus, God's Son, promises:

"And I give unto them eternal life; and they shall never perish, neither shall any man pluck them out of my hand."
JOHN 10:28

The Apostle Paul stated:

"For I am persuaded, that neither death, nor life, nor angels, nor principalities, nor powers, nor things present, nor things to come,

Nor height, nor depth, nor any other creature, shall be able to separate us from the love of God, which is in Christ Jesus our Lord."
ROMANS 8:38,39

14

☐ I'd like to know more about this New Life.

Please send me your *free* Bible study booklet so that I can discover how to have the full, abundant life God wants for me.

NAME _____
PLEASE PRINT

ADDRESS _____

CITY _____ STATE _____ ZIP_____

If you need further help, write:

15

HOW TO PRESENT THE GOSPEL

1. Show them their need of salvation (Romans 3:23; Romans 6:23; Isaiah 53:6).
2. Show them they cannot save themselves (Titus 3:5; Galatians 2:16; Proverbs 14:12).
3. Show them God's provision for their salvation (Romans 5:8; John 3:16; John 14:6; John 1:12).
4. Show them how to have the assurance of salvation (1 John 5:13; Romans 10:9; 1 John 1:9).
5. Show them that Jesus Christ will enable them to overcome temptation (2 Corinthians 5:17; 1 Corinthians 10:13).

VERSES TO COMMIT TO MEMORY

For all have sinned, and come short of the glory of God.
Romans 3:23

For the wages of sin is death; but the gift of God is eternal life through Jesus Christ our Lord.
Romans 6:23

All we like sheep have gone astray; we have turned every one to his own way; and the LORD hath laid on him the iniquity of us all.
Isaiah 53:6

Not by works of righteousness which we have done, but according to his mercy he saved us, by the washing of regeneration, and renewing of the Holy Ghost.
Titus 3:5

There is a way which seemeth right unto a man, but the end thereof are the ways of death.
Proverbs 14:12

For by grace are ye saved through faith; and that not of yourselves: it is the gift of God: Not of works, lest any man should boast.
Ephesians 2:8-9

But God commendth his love toward us, in that, while we were yet sinners, Christ died for us.
Romans 5:8

For God so loved the world, that he gave his only begotten Son, that whosoever believeth in him should not perish, but have everlasting life.
John 3:16

But as many as received him, to them gave he power to become the sons of God, even to them that believe on his name.

John 1:12

These things have I written unto you that believe on the name of the Son of God; that ye may know that ye have eternal life, and that ye may believe on the name of the Son of God.

1 John 5:13

Therefore if any man be in Christ, he is a new creature: old things are passed away; behold, all things are become new.

2 Corinthians 5:17

Jesus saith unto him, I am the way, the truth, and the life: no man cometh unto the Father, but by me.

John 14:6

That if thou shalt confess with thy mouth the Lord Jesus, and shalt believe in thine heart that God hath raised him from the dead, thou shalt be saved. For with the heart man believeth unto righteousness; and with the mouth confession is made unto salvation.

Romans 10:9-10

If we confess our sins, he is faithful and just to forgive us our sins, and to cleanse us from all unrighteousness.

1 John 1:9

Knowing that a man is not justified by the works of the law, but by the faith of Jesus Christ, even we have believed in Jesus Christ, that we might be justified by the faith of Christ, and not by the works of the law: for by the works of the law shall no flesh be justified.

Galatians 2:16

QUESTIONS

1. Why is it important to present the needs of salvation?
2. How does Isaiah 53:6 show man's need and God's provision for salvation?
3. Memorize Romans 3:23; Romans 6:23; Isaiah 53:6; John 3:16; Ephesians 2:8-9; and 1 John 5:13.
4. How would you present the fact that we cannot save ourselves? Back up your answer with Scripture.
5. Present God's provision for our salvation.
6. List three ways to overcome temptation.
7. How would you present the assurance of salvation?

71

I saw that it were better to make a mistake in one's first effort at personal religious conversation, and correct that mistake afterwards, than not to make any effort. There can be no mistake so bad, in working for an individual soul for Christ, as the fatal mistake of not making an honest endeavor. How many persons refrain from doing anything lest they possibly should do the wrong thing just now! Not doing is the worst of doing.

Henry Clay Trumbull, in
Individual Work for Individuals

7

MAY I BE EXCUSED?

"The man who is good for excuses," said Benjamin Franklin, "is good for little else." For literally millions of people, making excuses is a way of life. It is as common as taking a breath of air or going to sleep at night.

WHAT IS AN EXCUSE?

Most of us make excuses for all kinds of behavior. Some of the most common heard by ministers are the excuses for not coming to church. The weather keeps some away. Either it is too hot, too cold, too wet, or it is just *too nice.* Whatever the explanation, it really is only a coverup for indifference. In other words, it is an excuse.

What is an excuse? The dictionary defines it as any attempt "to regard or judge with indulgence . . . to pardon or forgive" one's actions.

It is my opinion that there is a considerable difference between a reason and an excuse. A *reason* is something we give, before a conclusion is reached. It is an underlying fact that provides logical sense for a decision or action. An *excuse* is something we give for not completing the action. Reasons are usually sincere. Excuses generally are rationalizations. A reason is reality, an excuse is an invention, or at best, a very, very weak reason.

WHY DO WE MAKE EXCUSES?

There are many reasons we excuse ourselves. There are probably as many reasons as there are people. But as we

73

examine closely this whole question, we discover several answers.

The Excuse of Lack of Ability

Some people make excuses because they lack confidence. Those people are often timid and shy. The Bible gives an illustration of this in Exodus 3. There we have the picture of Moses telling God of his inability to serve. In verse 11 we read, "And Moses said unto God, Who am I, that I should go unto Pharaoh, and that I should bring forth the children of Israel out of Egypt?"

Later, in Exodus 4, Moses tried to excuse himself with these words, "O my Lord, I am not eloquent, neither heretofore, nor since thou hast spoken unto thy servant; but I am slow of speech, and of a slow tongue. And the LORD said unto him, Who hath made man's mouth? or who maketh the dumb, or deaf, or the seeing, or the blind? have not I the LORD? Now therefore go, and I will be with thy mouth, and teach thee what thou shalt say" (Exodus 4:10-12).

Moses felt inferior. "The roof of my mouth gets dry," he seemed to say. "My tongue won't move, my knees knock. I am not eloquent. I can't be Your witness, Lord."

Can you sympathize with Moses? I have felt that way many times. Often I have questioned my abilities, my gifts, or the tools I have had to use, but the Lord seemed to say, "Go on, keep going on, and I will be with your mouth." Lay hold of that promise, and witness the best you know how.

It is not usually those who have the great gifts who get things done. D. L. Moody had only a fifth-grade education, but God used him to move two continents toward heaven. When God wants to get a job done, He doesn't usually look for a man or woman with tremendous talents or great abilities. He looks for a person who is dedicated to Him. When God made man, He used dirt, not diamonds. When He gave instructions for building the

74

tabernacle, He specified that it was to be built with boards and badger skins. God delights to use the simple things of life. God looks for someone who is willing to do anything, to go anywhere, to pay any price to accomplish His will. I find great comfort in the thought that "little is much when God is in it."

The best way to get started in witnessing is simply to *get started.* Start where you are, with what you have. Don't mull over all the pros and cons of the job. Don't analyze and alibi—start witnessing. The Lord will bless your efforts for Him no matter how feeble you might think them to be.

The Excuse of Blaming Others or Conditions

Shifting responsibility is also a common kind of excuse. Human beings for centuries have been trying to shift responsibility, to lay the blame on someone else. Go back to the very beginning. In Genesis 3, we are told about the failure of our first parents, Adam and Eve. In Genesis 3:9-13, we read, "And the LORD God called unto Adam, and said unto him, Where art thou? And he said, I heard thy voice in the garden, and I was afraid, because I was naked; and I hid myself. And he said, Who told thee that thou wast naked? Hast thou eaten of the tree, whereof I commanded thee that thou shouldest not eat? And the man said, The woman whom thou gavest to be with me, she gave me of the tree, and I did eat. And the LORD God said unto the woman, What is this that thou hast done? And the woman said, The serpent beguiled me, and I did eat."

Adam's first response was to blame Eve and God Himself. "The woman whom thou gavest . . . me, she gave me of the tree." Adam was using Eve as an excuse, but he was also blaming God. It is as if he were saying, "After all, Lord, You gave me this woman, it's really Your fault!"

Of course Eve was no better. She did the very same thing. In verse 13, she says, "The serpent beguiled." She also shifted the blame.

The real reason for Adam's and Eve's sin had nothing to do with those excuses. Verse 6 of the same chapter points out that when Eve looked upon the tree, she saw that it was good for food. She saw that it was pleasant to the eyes. She desired after it to make her wise. She yielded to the temptation and took the fruit. Adam and Eve used all kinds of excuses, but that's all they were—excuses! The root of their disobedience was selfishness.

A businessman told me that he could not witness because of an unsympathetic wife. I agreed that he should be loving and thoughtful to his wife, but suggested that he was really hiding behind his wife as an excuse. With a little thought and imagination, he could witness in many situations that would not involve his wife.

A woman told me that as a homemaker her opportunities were so limited that witnessing was impossible. I suggested inviting her neighbors in for a coffee time and fellowship or a cookies exchange, a Bible study, or just enclosing attractive tracts as she paid her bills. She was using her position in life as an excuse. If we sincerely want to witness, we can make opportunities. Too often we try to cover up by shifting the blame for our disobedience.

One of the most common examples of blame shifting is the person who says he is not a Christian or not a witnessing Christian because there are so many hypocrites in the church. What an empty excuse! That would be just like a dying man saying, "I would go to the hospital for help if there just weren't so many sick people there." Sad to say, there are some hypocrites in the church. There are some hypocrites in every area of life and every kind of organization. But it is dishonest to minimize the faithful, devoted people who are honestly serving and maximize those who are poor, insincere hypocrites.

Paul writes in Romans 14:12, "So then every one of us shall give account of himself to God." We will not have to answer for others. We will have to answer for ourselves! Are you ready? Are you prepared for that? Shifting the blame not only is weak and anemic, but it can be fatal as well.

The Excuse of Being Too Busy

"I'm doing too much already," is the excuse of some who merely play at being busy. But you know there is a difference between busyness and truly being busy. Some people may look and sound busy but in reality be totally unorganized. They waste a lot of time and fail to get things done. Others are lazy. They often excuse their own laziness by calling those with more ardent zeal fanatics.

But there is another group of people who truly *are* too busy. Jesus talked about them in His parable of the great supper (Luke 14). There, speaking to the religious leaders of His day, Jesus told the story of a man who planned a huge dinner party and invited many guests.

"Then said he unto him, A certain man made a great supper, and bade many: and sent his servant at supper time to say to them that were bidden, Come; for all things are now ready. And they all with one consent began to make excuse. The first said unto him, I have bought a piece of ground, and I must needs go and see it: I pray thee have me excused. And another said, I have bought five yoke of oxen, and I go to prove them: I pray thee have me excused. And another said, I have married a wife, and therefore I cannot come" (Luke 14:16-20).

I have several interesting observations. First, this supper was a special occasion; the guests had previously been invited. Verse 17 says that they "were bidden." The guests had been honored probably well in advance with an invitation to attend.

Second, we can rightly determine that these people who had been "bidden" to the feast were now just being summoned. In other words, these men had, in all likelihood, already consented to come. They were simply waiting for the announcement that the feast was ready to start.

77

Third, unfortunately we find that all three of the men excused themselves and refused to attend the dinner.

The first one said, "I have bought a piece of ground, and I must needs go and see it" (verse 18). What a weak excuse. If he had been a good businessman, he would have visited the land before he bought it. Furthermore, the fellow had already purchased the land; it was not going anywhere. He could just as well have visited his property *after* the dinner. He apparently was too involved with his possessions. But in reality, his answer was nothing more than an excuse, an excuse that held no credibility.

What did the second man say? He also excused himself because he was too busy. He had purchased five yoke of oxen, and he wanted to go prove them. This man's excuse was inadequate for the same reasons. Why had he not proven his animals before the dinner, or for that matter, why could they not wait until later? His excuse was, of course, just a lie.

But what about the third man? His excuse was the most ridiculous of all. He had just been married. This man, like the others, had promised ahead of time that he would attend. Could he not have brought his wife with him? The new bride might have enjoyed the banquet.

The fact illustrated by each of these men is that our feet follow our heart. Regardless of circumstances, people generally do what they want to do. That is what these men were doing in rejecting the offer to attend the feast.

People do what they want to do and make excuses for things they don't want to do.

WHAT DOES THE BIBLE SAY ABOUT EXCUSES?

Adam and Eve were judged and put out of the Garden of Eden. The master of the feast in Luke 14 was angry, and all those who made excuses were excluded—"none of those men which were bidden shall taste my supper" (Luke 14:24).

A familiar saying is that excuses satisfy only the people

who make them. And that is true. Consequently, when we excuse ourselves, we really accuse ourselves. Alexander Pope characterized excuses much more severely. "An excuse," he wrote, "is more terrible than a lie, for an excuse is a lie guarded." What he meant was that excuses are lies that masquerade as legitimate reasons, and therefore are doubly wrong.

But of course, the most important concern is what God thinks of our excuses. They do not satisfy Him. God expects us to serve Him faithfully. Just as the master of the feast was angry when his guests spurned him, so God is grieved and angry when we fail to obey Him, and excuse ourselves.

Remember that the God who calls us to witness also promises to give us strength for every situation (Philippians 4:13). "God is able to make all grace abound toward you" (2 Corinthians 9:8).

REMINDERS

- Reasons are usually sincere. Excuses are generally insincere rationalizations.
- When God made man, He used dirt, not diamonds. When He gave instructions for building the tabernacle, He specified that it was to be built with boards and badger skins.
- God delights to use the simple things of life.
- The best way to get started in witnessing is simply to get started.
- When we excuse ourselves, we really accuse ourselves.
- Excuses satisfy only the people who make them.
- "An excuse is more terrible than a lie, for an excuse is a lie guarded" (Alexander Pope).

QUESTIONS

1. What was God's answer to the excuse offered by Moses?
2. Is there a difference between an excuse and a reason? Illustrate your answer through the experience of Adam and Eve.

3. How would you answer the person who hides behind the excuse of hypocrisy? What Scripture would you use?
4. List the three excuses given in Luke 14 and why these answers were excuses.
5. What was the response of the master of the feast, and how do you imagine God feels about our excuses?
6. Quote two verses that constitute an answer to every possible excuse.

Isaiah lxvi. 8 tells us that "as soon as Zion travailed she brought forth her children"; and this is the most fundamental element in the work of God. Can children be born without pain? Can there be birth without travail? Yet how many expect in the spiritual realm that which is not possible in the natural!

Oswald J. Smith, in
The Passion for Souls

I think my soul was never so drawn out in intercession for others as it has been this night; I hardly ever so longed to live to God, and to be altogether devoted to Him; I wanted to wear out my life for Him.

I wrestled for the ingathering of souls, for multitudes of poor souls, personally, in many distant places.

The Journal of David Brainerd

8

A PASSION FOR SOULS

It is often said that if a man has a soul—and he has—and if that soul can be won or lost for eternity—and it can—the most important work in the world is to bring men and women to Jesus Christ.

The last words of Jesus while He was here on earth marked out our Christian responsibility, "Ye shall be witnesses unto me . . . unto the uttermost part of the earth" (Acts 1:8). The command was given by Jesus two thousand years ago, but it still applies today to each one who claims Christ as Saviour. To us has been given the privilege, yet the awesome responsibility, of telling the Good News to the world.

Before evangelism can ever be a program, it must be first a passion. If we are to witness for Christ successfully, we must honestly care for people.

It is important to feel and understand something of the love and concern of Christ for the people of the world. We must come to feel what God feels for those who are separated from Him. To possess a pleasing personality and Bible knowledge is very helpful, but it will accomplish very little apart from a divine passion.

John Henry Jowett wrote, "The gospel of a broken heart demands the ministry of bleeding hearts. . . . As soon as we cease to bleed, we cease to bless. . . . We can never heal the needs we do not feel. Tearless hearts can never be the heralds of the Passion." Pastor Jowett was writing about a "passion for souls."

Abraham, moved with a heart of love, prayed for the sake of a few righteous souls in Sodom and Gomorrah. Abraham knew something of the passion of God. "And Abraham drew near, and said, Wilt thou also destroy the righteous with the wicked? Peradventure there be fifty righteous within the city: wilt thou also destroy and not spare the place for the fifty righteous that are therein?" (Genesis 18:23-24).

Because Abraham could not find fifty righteous souls, he asked the Lord to withhold judgment for the sake of forty-five, and then forty, then thirty, then twenty; and finally he pleaded for the sake of ten souls. Abraham was moved by the passion of God.

God's servant Moses also experienced that kind of passion. Earnestly he prayed for the children of Israel, "Oh, this people have sinned a great sin, and have made them gods of gold. Yet now, if thou wilt forgive their sin—; and if not, blot me, I pray thee, out of thy book which thou hast written" (Exodus 32:31-32).

On that occasion, Moses so completely identified with Israel that he was willing to be forever blotted out of God's book, if by doing that they might be saved. Moses was overwhelmed with a passion for the souls of his people. What does it mean to have a passion for souls?

The word *passion* comes from the Latin word meaning "to suffer" or "to feel." The prefix "com" means "with." Therefore, *compassion* means "to suffer with" or "to feel with" others. A passion for souls is an attitude of compassion, a burning desire to see people saved. Our Lord Jesus was filled with compassion as He met and entered into the lives of the people of His day. At times He saw them as wandering sheep needing a shepherd. Matthew records, "He was moved with compassion on them" (Matthew 9:36). Jesus, seeing their tangled lives, loved them.

Do you view people with a heart of compassion? We all know what it is to feel inward pain for a loved one who is intensely ill. Jesus knew that emotion as well. He suffered within as He looked upon sick minds and bodies. Once, at least, He wept over Jerusalem as He saw their apparent unconcern. Lovingly He drew the little children to Himself. Out of a heart of mercy, He spoke gently to a fallen woman as He forgave her sins. And even as He was dying on the cross, He spoke words of tender compassion for those who had crucified Him. Jesus had compassion for people and so must we.

The apostle Paul also knew this deep inward passion. To the members of the church of Corinth, he wrote, "Out of much affliction and anguish . . . I wrote unto you with many tears" (2 Corinthians 2:4). Paul felt deeply about them. He suffered inwardly as he went with them through their sorrow.

To those in the church of Thessalonica he said, "Remember, brethren, our labour and travail: for labouring night and day, . . . we preached unto you the gospel" (1 Thessalonians 2:9).

Paul was so controlled with compassion—so constrained by the love of Christ—that he was willing to pour himself out in sharing the gospel with others. To the elders of the church at Ephesus he wrote, "Neither count I my life dear unto myself, so that I might finish . . . the ministry, which I have received of the Lord Jesus, to testify the gospel of the grace of God" (Acts 20:24).

Paul seldom did anything halfway. He was wholehearted when he persecuted the church, and he was equally committed in ministering for Christ in the church. He labored to build up the church he had formerly sought to destroy. Night and day he "ceased not to warn every one with tears" (Acts 20:31). Neither a dungeon nor chains nor physical beatings could remove the divine passion that was his. Paul served God and man from a heart of love, not because he pitied people, but rather because God had given him a divine passion.

Most of us, at least occasionally, pity the less fortunate or those living in ignorance in some remote part of the world. We may even shed a tear as we read of pain, hunger, and death, but once we enter into a "divine passion," we must serve, we must do something about it.

The most graphic illustration of Paul's passion for souls is found in his letter to the church at Rome. There we are given three aspects of the consuming passion that captured and controlled Paul. Notice that it was a sincere passion, a sorrowing passion, and a saving passion.

"I say the truth in Christ," writes Paul, "I lie not, my conscience also bearing me witness in the Holy Ghost, that I have great heaviness and continual sorrow in my heart. For I could wish that myself were accursed from Christ for my brethren, my kinsmen according to the flesh" (Romans 9:1-3). That is what "a passion for souls" is all about. What do we know of that kind of passion?

A SINCERE PASSION

Paul's passion for souls was for real. He said in essence, "I'm telling you the truth as a Christian, that I have great heaviness and continual sorrow in my heart." Paul's concern was a sincere passion.

Dr. C. E. Autrey says, "The keen observer can detect the difference between the mighty currents of passion for souls and foamy emotions. When the waves come in, there will always be some foam. Don't fear the foam if it is natural. Some emotion may be expected. We should wisely guard against the excesses. But let us not forget that spiritual lethargy and moral indifference are to be feared far more than emotion. Our danger today doesn't lie in the direction of uncontrolled emotionalism; it is in the realm of a cold, passionless Christianity."

How true! A witness must personally be moved by God before he will be moved to become involved with others.

The passion of Paul was no passing, sporadic, intermittent, emotional high. It was a deep, true, heartfelt concern. He had an abiding love for people, because he was in communion with Christ.

We see the sincerity of Paul's passion, expressed when he wrote, "Woe is unto me, if I preach not the gospel" (1 Corinthians 9:16). Wherever he was, he shared the gospel. In season and out of season, the consuming fire of his passion burned within him. Witnessing for Paul was not optional; he had to do it! He could not be silent. Paul's passion for souls was sincere. Paul was authentic.

A SORROWING PASSION

In Romans 9:2 we read, "I have great heaviness and continual sorrow in my heart." Because Paul's passion for souls was authentic, he apparently had the burden continually. Not only was there heaviness, there also were a great heaviness and continual sorrow whenever he considered the fate of his brethren without the gospel.

I wonder if we know anything about a sorrowing passion for people without God? Do we really care about others who pass on every day into a Christless eternity? If we really care, there will be times when we will scarcely be able to eat or sleep.

Paul's sorrowing passion was not just a hit-and-miss, now-and-then concern, it was constant. "I have continual sorrow in my heart," he declares. No wonder Paul wept, ceasing "not to warn every one night and day with tears" (Acts 20:31).

Are we familiar with that kind of concern? Someone has said that what we need is not primarily a passion for souls but a passion for Jesus Christ. That is true, for as we yield to Jesus Christ we will experience His divine desire to see men and women reconciled to God. As we come to know Jesus Christ, we will inevitably learn more of His passion for people.

87

A SAVING PASSION

In Romans 9:3, Paul states, "For I could wish that myself were accursed from Christ for my brethren, my kinsmen according to the flesh." He was saying that if by his own destruction he could see the salvation of his countrymen, he would gladly take their place. Like Moses, Paul was willing to identify himself totally with those he was seeking to win. It was the same kind of saving passion that gripped Henry Martyn, the great missionary to India, as he prayed, "Let me burn out for God."

A moving illustration of heartfelt concern and passion is seen in the life of Rachel, the wife of Jacob. The crowning glory of a Hebrew woman was to bear a child. Because Rachel was barren, her shame and concern deepened into a spirit of desperation. The Scripture reads, "And when Rachel saw that she bare Jacob no children, Rachel envied her sister; and said unto Jacob, Give me children, or else I die" (Genesis 30:1). But the Lord was very aware of Rachel's physical barrenness and answered her cry of desperation.

The prayer of John Knox was similar to Rachel's. It could well be that John Knox was moved to pray, "Lord, give me Scotland or else I die," because of Rachel's example. In both situations, God was pleased to respond miraculously to the cries of desperation.

Paul's passion was that his countrymen might be saved. In Romans 10:1, he expresses that purpose, "Brethren, my heart's desire and prayer to God for Israel is, that they might be saved."

Paul cared. His passion was a concern of the heart that resulted in action. Paul's one great burning desire was to see people brought to new life in Christ. To the church at Corinth he wrote, "I am made all things to all men, that I might by all means save some" (1 Corinthians 9:22).

Do we care? Are we expendable for God? Do we know something about a sincere, sorrowing, saving passion? This is not some magical thing. It is not simply the stirring of some emotional heartstrings. A passion for souls is a God-given concern to reach people with the good news of Christ.

REMINDERS

- "The gospel of a broken heart demands the ministry of a bleeding heart."

  J. H. Jowett
- "We can never heal the needs we do not feel."

  J. H. Jowett
- "Our danger today doesn't lie in the direction of uncontrolled emotionalism; it is in the realm of a cold, passionless Christianity."

  C. E. Autrey
- "And Moses returned unto the LORD, and said, Oh, this people have sinned a great sin, and have made them gods of gold. Yet now, if thou wilt forgive their sin—; and if not, blot me, I pray thee, out of thy book which thou hast written (Exodus 32:31-32).
- "And when Rachel saw that she bare Jacob no children, Rachel envied her sister; and said unto Jacob, Give me children or else I die" (Genesis 30:1).
- "I say the truth in Christ, I lie not, my conscience also bearing me witness in the Holy Ghost, that I have great heaviness and continual sorrow in my heart. For I could wish that myself were accursed from Christ for my brethren, my kinsmen according to the flesh" (Romans 9:1-3).

QUESTIONS

1. How did Abraham and Moses express their love for the people of their day?
2. Define the words *compassion* and *passion*. What do we mean by the phrase "a passion for souls"?
3. How was the reality of a passion for souls evident in the life of the apostle Paul?
4. Why did the apostle Paul experience a heaviness of heart?
5. What was the burning desire of Paul according to 1 Corinthians 9:22? Do you have that same desire?

People often ask, "If Christianity is true, why do the majority of intelligent people not believe it?" The answer is precisely the same as the reason the majority of unintelligent people don't believe it. They don't want to because they're unwilling to accept the moral demands it would make on their lives. We can take a horse to water but we can't make him drink. A person must be willing to believe before he ever will believe. There isn't a thing you or I can do with a man who, despite all evidence to the contrary, insists that black is white.

We ourselves must be convinced about the truth we proclaim. Otherwise we won't be at all convincing to other people. We must be able to say confidently with Peter, ". . . we did not follow cleverly devised myths when we made known to you the power and coming of our Lord Jesus Christ" (II Peter 1:16). Then our witness will ring with authority, conviction, and the power of the Holy Spirit.

Paul E. Little, in
How to Give Away Your Faith

Novelist Ayn Rand had mesmerized a student audience at Yale University with her prickly ideas. Afterward a reporter from *Time* magazine asked her, "Miss Rand, what's wrong with the modern world?"

Without hesitation she replied, "Never before has the world been so desperately asking for answers to crucial questions, and never before has the world been so frantically committed to the idea that no answers are possible.

"To paraphrase the Bible," she continued, "the modern attitude is, 'Father, forgive us, for we know not what we are doing—and *please don't tell us!*' "

It is to such a generation that God has called today's Christians to minister—in an age which sees everything that was nailed down coming loose, a time when things happen which people once thought could never happen.

Howard G. Hendricks, in
Say It with Love

9

HANDLING OBJECTIONS

To witness successfully, we must know why we believe as well as what we believe. Each Christian should be able to defend his faith. The Bible clearly tells us to "be ready always to give an answer to every man that asketh you a reason of the hope that is in you, with meekness and fear" (1 Peter 3:15).

No one can effectively share the gospel until he is convinced of its authority in his own mind and heart. Witnessing cannot be sustained for long unless the intellect agrees with the heart. In addition we have the privilege and responsibility to give answers to those who have honest objections.

I am not suggesting that we have all the answers. We do not. However, there are answers to some common questions that I would like to share with you.

"I DON'T BELIEVE THE BIBLE"

Occasionally as you begin witnessing, someone will respond, "I don't believe the Bible." Usually it is best to take that very objection as your starting point for a presentation of the gospel. Remember, however, that Peter and Paul taught and preached the Scriptures even though their hearers made no pretense of believing the Bible, whereupon the Holy Spirit took the Scriptures, and applied them so that many believed. Although we want to defend the faith intelligently, we should always remember that witnessing is primarily a proclamation of the faith.

When people say that the Bible is full of errors, often they are hiding behind a false objection. Usually I ask what particular passage of Scripture is troubling them. If I know the answer, I share it. If I do not, I tell them, "I don't know the answer, but I'll find the answer for you."

If the person objecting has read little of the Bible, you will soon realize that his objection is insincere. Under no circumstances, though, should we ever make light of a person's objections. Some passages of Scripture are difficult to answer. A knowledge of the surrounding verses often provides the answer.

Two forceful arguments are the transforming power of the Bible and the reliability of Scripture over the centuries. Continually archaeology confirms the Scripture.

"IS JESUS CHRIST THE ONLY WAY TO GOD?"

Often people feel that as long as an individual is sincere, God will be satisfied. In other words, the earnest Hindu or Muslim will be accepted because he, too, worships God, although under a different name.

But the issue is not how we view various religions, but what is truth. Sincerity is commendable, but it is not the deciding factor. For example, some religions recognize Jesus as a great teacher but not as the Son of God. They deny His deity, His atoning death, and His literal resurrection. Yet Jesus stated plainly in John 14:6, "I am the way, the truth, and the life: no man cometh unto the Father, but by me." According to Jesus Himself, there is no other way to God, and that is where the Christian must stand. It is not a matter of stubbornness but my response to divine truth as given in the Word of God.

"WHAT ABOUT THE HEATHEN?"

Some people reject the gospel because they cannot believe a righteous God can condemn people who have never heard the gospel. It is not an easy objection to answer. In attempting to answer their objection, three things must be kept in mind.

First, the Scriptures teach that God is just. We can have full confidence that whatever He does with those who have not heard the gospel will be fair. We must trust Him.

Second, God has spoken throughout history in many ways. One of those ways is creation. Romans 1:19-20 tells us that we are all without excuse. Why? "Because that which may be known of God is manifest in them; for God hath shewed it unto them. For the invisible things of him from the creation of the world are clearly seen, being understood by the things that are made, even his eternal power and Godhead; so that they are without excuse."

God has spoken to every man in creation and through the human conscience. To fail to respond to God's revelation makes one guilty.

Third, the final judgment will be based upon what each individual has done with Jesus Christ. The issue will not be the heathen, but what you have personally done with Jesus Christ. The Scriptures remind us that no one can come to the Father, except through Jesus Christ (John 14:6; Acts 4:12). That places considerable responsibility upon each believer. We must see to it that the unreached of our day hear the Good News.

"WOULD A GOD OF LOVE JUDGE MANKIND?"

Another common excuse for rejecting the gospel is the one given by people who refuse to believe that a God of love could condemn anyone. God is love, but He is also just and righteous. As such, He cannot allow sin or a sinful person in His presence. The prophet Habakkuk wrote, "Thou are of purer eyes than to behold evil, and canst not look on iniquity" (1:13). God loves all mankind, but when men and women neglect and reject God's love, they are the ones who separate themselves from God now and ultimately forever.

93

"I'M AFRAID I CAN'T HOLD OUT
AND LIVE THE CHRISTIAN LIFE."

Some people refuse to accept the gospel because they fear failure. No one can live the Christian life in his own strength. It is impossible. But when I received Jesus Christ, the Holy Spirit of God indwelt me (Ephesians 1:13; Romans 8:9). It is the Holy Spirit who keeps me going and gives me the power to go on with God. Without the enabling strength of God the Holy Spirit, I would fail.

"WHAT ABOUT THE MIRACLES OF THE BIBLE?"

Another excuse that people give for their unbelief is that they cannot believe some of the miracles of the Bible. My answer to the question of Bible miracles is found in the three-letter word God. If God is God, He has the ability to do anything. He is all-powerful. The Bible has proved itself trustworthy in the past, and there is good reason for trusting it in the present. God can and does intervene in the world that He has created.

"HOW DO YOU ACCOUNT FOR HUMAN SUFFERING?"

The Bible speaks of the suffering and despair of Job. In the depth of his experience he cried, "Why died I not from the womb? Why did I not give up the ghost when I came out of the belly?" (3:11). Job suffered the loss of wealth, family, and health. Each of us at times has probably asked, "Why? Why do we have wars? Why are some born blind and others dumb? If God is all-powerful, why does He permit evil?"

I do not believe anyone can fully answer those questions, and we ought to say so. However, let me suggest some areas to consider.

The Scriptures teach that God created a perfect world, which was marred by the entrance of sin (Genesis 3:14-15). All suffering is directly or indirectly related to the Fall of man. Because man violated God's law, evil exists in the world.

Added to that is the fact that we are individuals with the power of choice. We can choose good or evil. We are not robots. Often suffering is the result of our rebellious wills (Genesis 1:26-27; 3:6-13). Within God's sovereignty, we can choose and reap the fruits of our choices. David chose Bathsheba and reaped the consequences. Much of the suffering in this world is the result of our choices.

Then, too, there are times when suffering appears to be for the glory of God, as illustrated in John 9:1-3. Believers in Christ often claim His promise of Romans 8:28, "And we know that all things work together for good to them that love God, to them who are the called according to his purpose." Suffering at times may not appear to benefit me for the moment, yet I can rest in the knowledge that the experience is for my ultimate good. C. S. Lewis reminds us that it is foolish to speculate about the origin of evil. Rather, we should recognize the fact of evil and recognize that the only solution is found in Jesus Christ.

"WON'T GOD FORGIVE ME IF I LIVE A GOOD MORAL LIFE?"

For God to forgive sin without dealing with it would be totally contrary to His nature and righteous rule. God is holy. "Justice and judgment are the habitation of thy throne" (Psalm 89:14).

Also, the Bible teaches, "All our righteousnesses are as filthy rags" (Isaiah 64:6). "So then they that are in the flesh cannot please God" (Romans 8:8). The Bible teaches that a good moral life falls short of what God requires (Romans 3:23). No morality or work of ours could ever merit God's forgiveness or make us acceptable. Sin must be dealt with and removed. That is only possible through the atoning death of Jesus Christ.

At times I have been unable to give what might be called a satisfying answer. Yet substantial progress was made by being a concerned listener and showing genuine interest. Always remember that the agnostics and atheists face many unanswered questions.

A graduate from the University of Moscow and life-long Communist committed himself to Christ. When I asked him what convinced him more than anything else to become a Christian, he answered, "The love and interest of other Christians."

May we "be ready always to give an answer" (1 Peter 3:15), but also remember that "faith cometh by hearing and hearing by the word of God" (Romans 10:17).

SOME THINGS FOR THE WITNESS TO REMEMBER

As the soul winner presses this battle to the heart of the lost person in soulful compassion, let him remember:

1. Christ and his Spirit are with him, even by his side and within his very heart. He aids, he loves, he longs, he intercedes for him and for the sinner. He presses with him and through him his message. You are not alone. He says, "I am with you when you go to make disciples and teach them."

2. Remember his Word is powerful, sharper than any two-edged sword. His gospel is the power of God unto salvation and it will not return void. It will accomplish that for which he sent it.

3. Remember that no case is too hard for Christ and his gospel. "He is able to save unto the uttermost all them that come unto God by him." Have faith in Christ and his truth.

4. Remember that it is Christ and his gospel that save. You cannot save the soul of anyone . . . sentiment and tear-stories won't save. Christ will. Do not deceive the sinner. Do not give him a stone for bread. He needs Christ, only Christ, all of Christ, and Christ offers himself through you.

5. Remember that "faint heart never won fair lady." Be bold, be brave, persistent, kindly, patient. Do not give up easily. Your adversary the devil never gives up.

George Muller kept on sixty-two years after one man and won him. I know a wife who prayed every day for forty years for her husband and won him. You can win. God says we shall reap if we faint not.

6. Remember the prize is worth the noblest effort. You deal with immortal souls, dear to God, to Christ, and to you. If I were to live a thousand years and win one soul to Christ, my life would have been immeasurably worth while if I did nothing else; but I should win souls every day, whether I live long or short. If I had ten thousand lives, I would give every one of them full-length for winning souls and serving Christ.

L. R. Scarborough, in
A Search for Souls

10

SEEKING A VERDICT

From Genesis to Revelation, the hand of God reaches out to welcome men and women. The book of Genesis pictures God calling to Noah, "Come thou and all thy house into the ark" (Genesis 7:1). Someone has taken the time to count the word *come* in the Bible. It is used more than 600 times. God is so interested in our salvation that through direct invitation, by parables, types, and symbols, He continually calls. The New Testament says of Jesus, "The Son of man is come to seek and to save that which was lost" (Luke 19:10). The Bible also ends with a loving, urgent, all-inclusive call, "The Spirit and the bride say, Come. And let him that heareth say, Come. And let him that is athirst come. And whosoever will, let him take the water of life freely" (Revelation 22:17).

When we witness we have a responsibility to proclaim God's invitation and ask for a verdict. It is not only our responsibility to declare what God has done through Jesus Christ; we must tell also what He expects of men and women and seek a verdict.

WHY SHOULD WE SEEK A VERDICT?

We have the constant example of Scripture in seeking a verdict. As we review the ministry of God's servants in the Bible, we discover a common characteristic in their dealings with people. Notice just a few illustrations.

While Moses was receiving the Law, the children of

Israel became restless and rebellious. Their dissatisfaction resulted in careless conduct and idolatry. They ate, drank, and corrupted themselves in idolatrous worship (Exodus 32:7). When Moses returned and saw their idolatry, he became angry. He burned the golden calf they were worshiping, ground it to powder, and threw the ashes upon the waters. The next day Moses called the people together and pressed them for a verdict. "Then Moses stood in the gate of the camp, and said, Who is on the LORD'S side? let him come unto me" (Exodus 32:26).

Joshua, the successor of Moses, also sought a verdict. At Shechem he challenged the people, "Choose you this day whom ye will serve" (Joshua 24:15). And the people responded. It is interesting to observe that Joshua recorded the decision of the people in the book of the Law of God (Joshua 24:26) and then erected a "decision card" of stone as a witness to their response (24:27).

King Josiah also called upon the children of Israel to renew their vows to the Lord. He challenged them "to keep his commandments, and his testimonies, and his statutes, with all his heart, and with all his soul, to perform the words of the covenant" (2 Chronicles 34:31).

But Josiah even went a step further. The next verse reads, "He caused all that were present . . . to stand to it" (2 Chronicles 34:32). Josiah felt that his witness was incomplete until there was a definite affirmation of purpose. Josiah sought a verdict. Ezra and Nehemiah did the same. The Scriptures abound with examples of God's servants seeking a verdict.

Jesus also set an example for us. He came saying, "Repent ye, and believe the gospel" (Mark 1:15). To Peter and Andrew he called, "Come ye after me, and I will make you to become fishers of men" (Mark 1:17). Jesus continually sought a verdict. He pressed for a decision.

Howard Hendricks has written, "The entire New Testament is a record of the continuing entreaty of the Lord toward a world He had already died to redeem. God didn't just *say*, 'Be saved'; He said it with the highest degree of love."[1]

Staggering though it may seem, God is calling people through you and me today. Charles B. Williams translates 2 Corinthians 5:20, "So I am an envoy to represent Christ, because it is through me that God is making His appeal. As one representing Christ I beg you, be reconciled to God." We must realize that the great, Almighty God is calling men and women through what we are, say, and do.

Someone might ask, "Is it really right to attempt to persuade a person to receive Jesus Christ?" I believe it is. But we should remember that although Jesus sought sinners, He never forced anyone to follow Him. In Mark 10:17, we are told that Jesus, seeing the rich young ruler, "loved him" (Mark 10:21). Yet, when this man turned away, Jesus did not run after him. Jesus did not stiff-arm his way into his life. Our Lord spoke with him and loved him, but He did not force him to respond.

The apostle Paul used all his God-given wisdom and logic to bring those to whom he witnessed to the place of decision. On one occasion Paul wrote, "Knowing therefore the terror of the Lord, we persuade men" (2 Corinthians 5:11). A study of the book of Acts presents Paul as a serious persuader. Paul apparently believed in seeking a verdict.

WHY IS IT THAT SOME HESITATE TO SEEK A VERDICT?

Let me suggest several reasons some people hesitate to seek a verdict or actively persuade people to accept Christ.

Misunderstanding

Some people feel there is a logical inconsistency between God's sovereignty and human responsibility. Most of us at some time or other have wrestled with the problem. At times it is extremely difficult to know where the

---

[1]Howard G. Hendricks, *Say It with Love* (Wheaton, Ill.: Victor, 1972). p. 15.

Spirit stops and the flesh begins. It is a serious and sensitive area.

James I. Packer writes in *Evangelism and the Sovereignty of God,* "We must recognize that there is an apparent incompatibility between God's sovereignty and human responsibility. We cannot solve it. We must learn to live with it. We must avoid the temptation either to an exclusive concern with human responsibility or to an exclusive concern with divine sovereignty which makes us cynical about all evangelistic endeavors."

Occasionally someone will suggest that since the unconverted are dead spiritually and dead people cannot respond, believers should not try to persuade them. But is it true that we should not ask people to do what they cannot do? Jesus called Lazarus, who was dead, and the dead man did what he could not do; Lazarus came forth (John 11:44). Jesus told the impotent man, "Rise, take up thy bed, and walk," and he did (John 5:8). To the man with the withered hand, Jesus said, "Stretch forth thine hand," and the man responded (Mark 3:5).

Always remember that the God who calls men and women to come also enables them to come. As representatives of Jesus Christ, Almighty God calls to men to make a decision through you and me. That is an awesome truth.

Fear

Some might neglect to seek a verdict because of fear. Fear of failure or of rejection is very real. But when we realize the message we have, the value of a soul, the blessedness of heaven, and the reality of hell, we dare not allow fear to keep us from seeking decisions. As witnesses, we need to pray that the seed will fall upon responsive soil and then do all we can to seek a verdict.

Fatigue

It is possible to expend all of our thoughts and efforts in preparation and presentation and fail to prepare for the closing moments of decision. When we consider the ministry we have, however, all other considerations must be laid aside. Philip the deacon (Acts 8) followed through until the Ethiopian was fully satisfied; "he went on his way rejoicing" (Acts 8:39). By all means, give your finest thoughts and efforts to the strategic moment of decision.

HOW SHOULD WE SEEK A VERDICT?

Let me suggest several things to keep in mind as you seek a verdict.

Seek a verdict lovingly.

"[Love] shall cover the multitude of sins" (1 Peter 4:8). Love also can cover the mistakes we make in witnessing. We will not be offensive if we are mastered by the love of Jesus Christ. Divine love is not crude or rude. Love is considerate and always courteous. Be channels of God's love so that the Holy Spirit can love through you (Romans 5:5).

Seek a verdict believingly.

The element of faith is very important. The Bible says that "without faith it is impossible to please [God]" (Hebrews 11:6). The combination of love and faith is life-changing, and each witness should earnestly cultivate both of those gifts. The overwhelming evidence of Scripture as well as the example of Jesus encourage us to seek a verdict.

REMINDERS

- From Genesis to Revelation, the loving hand of God reaches out to seek and save men and women.
- It is interesting to observe that Joshua recorded the decision of the people in the book of the Law of God (Joshua 24:26) and then erected a "decision card" of stone as a witness to their response (Joshua 24:27).
- It is not only our responsibility to share and declare what God has done through Jesus Christ, we must

---

also tell what God expects of men and women.
- Although Jesus sought sinners, He never coerced anyone.

- "We must recognize there is an apparent incompatibility between God's sovereignty and human responsibility. We cannot solve it. We must learn to live with it. We must avoid the temptation either to an exclusive concern with human responsibility or to an exclusive concern with divine sovereignty which makes us cynical about all evangelistic endeavors" (James I. Packer).

- The overwhelming testimony of Scripture, as well as the example of Jesus, indicate that by all means we should seek a verdict.

QUESTIONS

1. Relate how Moses and Joshua sought a verdict.
2. Through whom does God make His appeal today according to 2 Corinthians 5:20?
3. Did Paul attempt to persuade people to believe in Jesus Christ? Support your answer with Scripture.
4. What do we mean when we say there is an apparent incompatibility between God's sovereignty and human responsibility?
5. Suggest two possible reasons believers often fail to seek a verdict.
6. Discuss the importance of seeking a verdict lovingly and believingly.

Much of the work of discipling has not included that of teaching; and much of the work of teaching has ignored that of discipling.

John A. Broadus

Henry Ford, the father of "mass production," is reported to have made the statement: "You can have any color Ford you want as long as it's black." His mass-producing manufacturing process required that everything be made exactly alike. While it is the goal of Christian nurture that each Christian be "Christ-like," we must keep in mind that Christian lives are not mass produced. It takes months instead of minutes to establish a lasting Christian life . . . months (sometimes years) of painstaking, "hot-house" nursery vigilance and care of the seeds sown and/or reaped by evangelism.

D. James Kennedy, in
Evangelism Explosion

11

THE IMPORTANCE OF FOLLOW-UP

One of our greatest areas of weakness is the following up of new believers. Great effort is put forth in witnessing and bringing friends to the place of decision, but too often they are neglected once they have received Christ. It is very important to conserve each decision. Too often we drift into an attitude of carelessness and imagine that the new Christian will automatically grow into a mature believer. Let me suggest some guidelines for follow-up.

USE A DECISION CARD

I have found that it is helpful to formulate a paragraph that states simply and clearly the decision that has been made. It should be written down and kept as a reminder to the person who has received Christ.

When Joshua challenged the people of Israel in his final message, he called upon them to make a definite decision. After the people made their decision to serve and obey the Lord, Joshua wrote it in a book.

> And Joshua wrote these words in the book of the law of God, and took a great stone, and set it up there under an oak, that was by the sanctuary of the LORD (Joshua 24:26).

So that the people would never forget it, Joshua erected a "decision card" of stone.

> This stone shall be a witness unto us; for it hath heard all the words of the LORD which he spake unto us: it shall be therefore a witness unto you (Joshua 24:27).

The Bible teaches that when you place your faith in Jesus Christ, you are born again by the "word of God" (1 Peter 1:23). A decision card could be compared to a spiritual *birth certificate*. It is a reminder of your commitment to Jesus Christ. The decision card might be worded like this:

Today,_____, I asked Jesus Christ to be my personal Saviour. The best I know how, I have committed my life to Him for forgiveness of all my sins and for His will for my life in the future. To the best of my ability, in dependence upon the Lord, I shall seek to witness to others concerning Jesus Christ.

Encourage the new believer to keep it in his wallet or purse as a lifelong reminder of his decision.

USE HELPFUL LITERATURE

Another helpful thing to do in following up new believers is to supply them with sound, helpful literature. Years ago, out of a sense of wanting to do more for new believers, I wrote this tract, which is available from Moody Press.

I am so happy for your decision to accept Christ as your Saviour, Lord, and Master. The Bible says, "Except a man be born again, he cannot see the kingdom of God" (John 3:3). Because you have committed yourself to Christ, you have become a child of God and He has become your heavenly Father.

As a newborn child is cared for in the physical world, so you must be helped and instructed in spiritual matters.

First, you should *read the Bible* systematically. The gospel of John is a good place for you to begin. What food is to the body, the Bible is to the soul. At a prescribed time in a quiet place, each day should start with the Bible. This is a must if you are to grow in the things of God. Remember, at least a chapter a day. "The Bible will keep you from sin, or sin will keep you from the Bible."

Second, you must learn to *pray*. Prayer is the communion of the believer with God. We speak to God but He also speaks to us. Prayer is not merely asking favors of God but rather waiting in quietness before Him. Pray for personal cleansing and victory over evil. Pray for yourself and pray for others.

Third, you are to use every opportunity to *confess Christ* before the world. In a cheerful way, immediately tell someone of your spiritual decision. Activity always strengthens. When God's people witness to others, they develop a big appetite for Bible study. The result of their speaking to others of their new life will provide daily up-to-date subjects for prayer. When a new convert begins to share his faith, everything comes into proper focus. "If you make a great deal of Christ, He will make a great deal of you; but if you make but little of Christ, Christ will make but little of you."

Fourth, you should *find a church home*. If a mother permits her children to grow up in idleness, the result will be untaught children. Since the Christian's duty is evident in this matter, waiting only forms bad habits. The Bible says, "Not forsaking the assembling of ourselves together as the manner of some is" (Hebrews 10:25). Your faithful church attendance will help you in spiritual growth, Christian education, missions, and social outreach.

If you follow these four Bible principles, Christian growth is guaranteed. Doubtless you will meet with temptations; but you need not yield or fall, for God has promised, "Greater is he that is in you, than he that is in the world" (1 John 4:4). *If you fall*, seek immediate forgiveness. "If we confess our sins, he is faithful and just to forgive us our sins, and to cleanse us from all unrighteousness" (1 John 1:9). Do not remain defeated; get up and go right on. Perhaps you are facing the battle of some habit: remember that Christ is ready to help you, and He has all power in heaven and earth.

In short, the secret of successful Christian living is to *keep your eyes on Christ*. The best of men will fail you at times, but Jesus Christ never fails.

At times it is only possible to follow up a person with a simple tract. However, in most cases, we can follow up with substantial literature and books.

To help meet the needs of the new believer, I wrote *How to Begin the Christian Life,* with a leader's guide to accompany it. Both are available from Moody Press. Many good books to help the new Christian are available. Be sure the ones you select are sound yet simple enough for the new Christian to understand.

APPOINT A SPIRITUAL GUARDIAN

Although a person may receive the Lord Jesus Christ in a relatively short period of time, a lifetime is involved in becoming like Jesus Christ. The goal for each new believer is to be conformed to the image of Jesus Christ (Romans 8:29).

Christians are not mass produced. Just as a baby requires painstaking care, plenty of love, and constant attention, so each new believer needs tender love and care. There must be that personal touch in follow-up. To be effective, follow-up should be personal, persistent, and purposeful.

Letters and literature are helpful, but nothing compares with the loving care of another Christian. Follow-up is most effective when it is personal.

Follow-up should also be persistent. Although it can be abused, persistence usually conveys that there is a deep, abiding interest. A loving persistence so often makes a difference.

By "purposeful," I mean our follow-up should lead into the fellowship of a local church.

Here is a checklist for the guardian:
1. Pray for the one you've been assigned to each day.
2. Warmly welcome him into your fellowship or group.
3. Visit him in his home. Observe his interests. Be aware of his likes and dislikes. Learn his special talents.

110

4. Arrange to sit with him in church if wise and possible.
5. Seek to introduce him into some other church function.
6. Invite him into your home.
7. Provide guidance for him in the Christian life.
8. Carefully notice any indications of error and attempt to correct him lovingly.

INTRODUCE THE NEW BELIEVER TO THE CHURCH

There is nothing on earth that is more significant in the growth of each believer than the church. It is true that although the church has many critics, it has no rival. Jesus Christ is the foundation of the church (Ephesians 1:22-23) and He has guaranteed its future (Matthew 16:18).

Environment is so very important. A tulip bulb on the sidewalk will not grow. If the bulb is placed in the soil, it has a promising future. Each new believer needs the fellowship of a local church and the friendship of God's people. The Bible simply says, "not forsaking the assembling of ourselves together, as the manner of some is" (Hebrews 10:25). This verse specifically warns us against neglect of assembling with fellow believers.

In *How to Begin the Christian Life*, I deal with the church. Permit me to include these paragraphs:

> Actually, the Greek word *ekklesia*, which is translated "church" in the New Testament, refers to either a local assembly of Christian believers or else to the universal Body of Christ made up of all people everywhere who have received Jesus Christ as Saviour. In 1 Corinthians 1:2 we read, '. . . all that in every place call upon the name of Jesus Christ our Lord.' This refers to the *mystical Body* of Christ, often called the *Bride of Christ*, or the Church universal.
>
> However, this same verse begins, "Unto the church of God which is at Corinth." This plainly refers to the *local congregation* of believers at Corinth.
>
> The word *ekklesia* is made up of two separate words,

111

the preposition *ek* meaning "out of," and the verb *kaleo*, meaning "to call." The Church is *a called-out group of people*, a people separated by God unto Himself. . . .

When the word *ekklesia* or *church* is found in the New Testament, it generally refers to a body of believers banded together in a definite place; in other words, a particular group of people organized in a local community, accepting the Scriptures as the basis of faith and conduct.

P. T. Forsythe spoke of the local church as the "outcrop of the church universal." The local church is vital and is God's means of accomplishing His work here on earth.

As soon as possible, the new believer should be introduced to the opportunities and responsibilities of the local church. It could be through an orientation class, the Sunday school, or even an informal Bible study group from the church.

The task of the church is more than evangelization. It includes worship, encouragement, edification, training, fellowship, and world outreach. The great commission stresses "teaching them to observe all things whatsoever I have commanded you" (Matthew 28:20). We must not only reach but teach and enlist.

New military recruits are enlisted and trained for the conflict. So we, too, must instruct each new believer to be ready for the battles of life. Through neglect, many new Christians are lost to fruitfulness even though their souls have been saved.

REMINDERS

- So that the people would never forget it, Joshua erected a "decision card" of stone as a memorial.
- A decision card is a kind of spiritual birth certificate.
- Christians are not mass produced. Just as a baby requires painstaking care, plenty of love, and loads of attention, so each believer needs tender love and care.
- Although the church has many critics, it has no rival.

QUESTIONS

1. Why is a decision card helpful?
2. Discuss the responsibilities of a spiritual guardian?
3. How should a new believer be received?
4. Define the word *church*.
5. Define the universal church and local church using 1 Corinthians 1:2.
6. What are some of the responsibilities of the church to its members?

Samuel Zwemer once addressed a student convention on the needs of the Islamic world, and closed his appeal by walking over to a great map of the Muslim lands. Spreading his arms over it, he said, "Thou, O Christ, art all I need; and Thou, O Christ, art all they need."

He is our urgency.

Leighton Ford, in
The Christian Persuader

I believe that if an angel were to wing his way from earth up to Heaven, and were to say that there was one poor, ragged boy, without father or mother, with no one to care for him and teach him the way of life; and if God were to ask who among them were willing to come down to this earth and live here for fifty years and lead that one to Jesus Christ, every angel in Heaven would volunteer to go. Even Gabriel, who stands in the presence of the Almighty, would say, "Let me leave my high and lofty position, and let me have the luxury of leading one soul to Jesus Christ." There is not greater honor than to be the instrument in God's hands of leading one person out of the kingdom of Satan into the glorious light of Heaven.

D. L. Moody

12

GOD'S HURRY

Have you ever thought of Almighty God as being in a
hurry? Probably not. Usually, we think of God as having
little or no concern with time. And yet, a note of urgency
runs through the entire Bible. Is God ever in a hurry?

During His earthly ministry, Jesus gave an illustration
that tells something of God's concern for the souls of
people. While speaking to a crowd of religious leaders,
He told the story of the prodigal son (Luke 15). That
young man rebelled against his father and is an illustration of all men and women. The prodigal son is a picture
of a prodigal world. Indifferent to his father's will, the son
insisted on his own way of riotous living. Ultimately he
squandered his inheritance, recognized his sin, and decided to return to his father and home.

The father in this passage is a picture of the heavenly
Father waiting and even looking for His son's return. The
Scripture says, "But when he was yet a great way off, his
father saw him, and had compassion, and ran, and fell on
his neck, and kissed him" (Luke 15:20).

The father's eyes of love were swifter than the feet of
repentance. He saw his son, had compassion, and ran to
welcome him home. The father was in a hurry to receive
his wayward son.

J. B. Phillips translates verses 22-24 as, " 'Hurry!' called
out his father to the servants, 'fetch the best clothes and

put them on him! Put a ring on his finger and shoes on his feet, and get that fatted calf and kill it, and we will have a feast and a celebration! For this is my son—he was dead, and he's alive again.' " The father not only hurried to receive his son, but demanded haste in preparing the celebration of restoration.

On one occasion, Jesus said, "I must work the works of him that sent me, while it is day: the night cometh, when no man can work" (John 9:4). Even though Jesus was God, He was aware of the limitations of time. Surely, we humans have only a few short years to witness and then the night will come. Our witnessing days will not last forever.

But there are other references in Scripture that illustrate the necessity of divine haste:

THE RESURRECTION

Although Jesus repeatedly told His disciples of His coming resurrection, they apparently were unprepared. On the resurrection morning, God's angel appeared and spoke to the woman at the tomb. "He is not here: for he is risen, as he said. Come, see the place where the Lord lay. And go quickly, and tell his disciples that he is risen from the dead" (Matthew 28:6-7).

"Go quickly." How were the women to go? The message of the resurrection demanded a holy haste.

THE EARLY CHURCH

When the angel of the Lord directed Philip the deacon to witness to the Ethiopian eunuch, "Philip ran thither to him" (Acts 8:30).

Paul teaches that believers must "Redeem the time, because the days are evil" (Ephesians 5:16). He encouraged young Timothy: "Stir up the gift of God, which is in thee" (2 Timothy 1:6). Paul was saying, "Fight the fading flame; don't get cold." I have noticed that a hot fire burns easily, but a weak one struggles all the way.

Coming to the last book of the Bible, we hear the call to readiness and witness. "Behold, I come quickly: hold that fast which thou hast, that no man take thy crown" (Revelation 3:11).

J. I. Packer pointedly comments, "Whatever we may believe about election, the fact remains that men without Christ are lost, and going to hell . . . 'Except ye repent,' said our Lord to the crowd, 'ye shall all . . . perish.' And we who are Christ's are sent to tell them of the One—the only One—who can save them from perishing. Is not their need urgent? . . . does that not make evangelism a matter of urgency for us?"[1]

The words of instruction and warning in Revelation 3:11 are followed with the illustration of a lukewarm church that had lost its urgency.

An Alarm Is Sounded

"I know thy works, that thou art neither cold nor hot: I would thou were cold or hot. So then because thou art lukewarm, and neither cold nor hot, I will spue thee out of my mouth" (Revelation 3:15-16).

"You are lukewarm, neither cold nor hot." A sleeping church is no contest for a red hot world. A comfortable, cozy Christian in Sleepy Valley will not evangelize the world.

Jesus is saying, "Wake up! Work while it is day."

The greatest problem facing the church today is the number of lukewarm, uninvolved Christians who fail to witness concerning Jesus Christ. At times it seems as though some believers have a mild case of Christianity and respond as though they've been vaccinated against the real thing. In a world on fire, lukewarmness will fail. In fact, lukewarmness is nauseating to God.

What happened 1200 years ago to the church in North Africa? It failed to be a mission force and today it is a mission field. What happened to the church in Russia a half century ago? Saltless, tasteless, and lightless, it be-

---

[1]J. I. Packer, *Evangelism & the Sovereignty of God* (Downers Grove, Ill.: InterVarsity, 1961), p. 98.

came ineffective. Having no sense of urgency, those churches drifted into death.

A farmer was awakened in the middle of the night when his clock struck seventeen times. Confused, he rushed all over the house waking everybody up shouting, "Get up! Get up! It's later than it ever has been before!"

In reality, it's later than it ever has been before. Are we ready and able to meet the challenge?

An Assessment Is Made

The trouble with the church at Laodicea is found in two phrases, "Thou sayest . . . and knowest not" (verse 17). Those are not pretty words and there is no way to make them attractive.

"Because thou sayest, I am rich, and increased with goods, and have need of nothing; and knowest not that thou art wretched, and miserable, and poor, and blind, and naked" (Revelation 3:17). That is not the assessment of a man, but of an all-knowing God. God forbid that it should be true of us.

Action Is Required

"As many as I love, I rebuke and chasten: be zealous therefore and repent. Behold, I stand at the door, and knock: if any man hear my voice, and open the door, I will come in to him, and will sup with him, and he with me" (Revelation 3:19-20).

"Be zealous therefore." The word *zealous* means "active, devoted, fervent, passionate, warm, and enthusiastic."

"You lack a sense of urgency," Jesus is saying. "You show little compassion. It is now time to repent!"

Commenting on this verse and the word *repent*, the famous preacher Alexander MacLaren told his congregation that in repentance "there must be a lowly consciousness of sin, a clear vision of past shortcomings . . . an abhorrence of these, and joined with that, a resolute act of

118

mind and heart beginning a new course, and a change of purpose."

In other words, repentance means more than just feeling deep sorrow about the past; real repentance leads to action.

Archbishop William Temple once said, "When people complain that the church should do something, they usually mean that the pastor should say something." Our sin has been that we talk too much and do too little.

It is time that we who are a part of the church of Jesus Christ begin to feel and understand God's hurry. That little couplet is true, "Only one life, 'twill soon be past. Only what's done for Christ will last."

The time to witness is now—not tomorrow or next month, or next year—it is now! Our world is red hot with need. Millions of men and women are lost and on their way to a Christless eternity unless you and I do something about it—unless we share God's salvation.

Every old-time circus had a barker who promoted each attraction. He would call out, "Hurry! Hurry! Hurry!" And people would hasten to some trivial and carnal event.

At times, I seem to hear an inner voice calling, "Hurry! Hurry! Hurry, for those I love die so fast." The call is not to some earthly side event, but to the main issue of time and eternity. Even now I sense the Holy Spirit calling, "Be zealous. Stir up the gift. Redeem the time. Work while it is day. Hurry! Hurry! Hurry!"

REMINDERS

- I have noticed that a hot fire burns easily, but a weak one struggles all the way.
- A comfortable, cozy Christian in Sleepy Valley will never evangelize the world.
- At times it seems as though some believers have a mild case of Christianity, and respond as though they've been vaccinated against the real thing.

119

- "When people complain that the church should do something, they usually mean that the pastor should say something" (Archbishop William Temple).

- Only one life, 'twill soon be past,
  Only what's done for Christ will last.

- At times, I sense the inner voice of God calling, "Hurry! Hurry! Hurry, for those I love die so fast."

QUESTIONS

1. List at least four Bible examples of urgency.
2. What ways can you think of to "redeem the time" (Ephesians 5:16) or to "stir up the gift of God" (2 Timothy 1:16)?
3. What was the problem of the Laodicean church, according to Revelation 3:16?
4. What two phrases in Revelation 3:17 further identify the condition of this church?
5. Define the word *zealous*. How can we encourage zeal?

Love this world through me, Lord
This world of broken men,
Thou didst love through death, Lord
Oh, love in me again!
Souls are in despair, Lord.
Oh, make me know and care;
When my life they see,
May they behold Thee,
Oh, love the world through me.

Dr. Will Houghton
Fourth president of Moody Bible Institute

I took up that word "Love," and I do not know how many weeks I spent in studying the passages in which it occurs, till at last I could not help loving people. It just flowed out my fingertips.

D. L. Moody, quoted in
Bush Aglow by R. E. Day

Yes, love is the magic key of life—not to get what we want but to become what we ought to be.

Eileen Guder

Do you know the world is dying
For a little bit of love?
Everywhere we hear them sighing,
For a little bit of love.

Anonymous

13

WITNESSING BEGINS WITH LOVE

During my student days at the Moody Bible Institute, I was seriously ill. Our school doctor, Titus Johnson, recommended immediate surgery for the removal of a tumor. Because it appeared to be malignant, the operation was followed by 30 X-ray treatments. I shall always remember the loving, honest concern of missionary doctor Titus Johnson. Carefully he explained that my condition could be fatal, and if not, the possibilities of my fathering children were remote.

My hospital bed at the Swedish Covenant Hospital was, in a real sense, my altar. I reminded the Lord of my desire to serve Him. I told him that I wanted His will more than anything in this life. I prayed, "Dear Lord, this hospital bed is my altar of sacrifice. If it is according to your will, let me be a living sacrifice. In a new way, I yield my life to you. In Jesus' name, amen."

During those days, a former Sunday school teacher sent me a booklet by James McConkey on the theme of God's love. As I read it, I began to see my need in this specific area. The combination of sickness, the quietness of the hospital, the booklet about God's love, the possibilities of death, were blended by the Great Physician to make me conscious of the supreme importance of God's love. Through it all, I caught a glimmer of the preeminence of God's love and the exciting possibility of becoming a channel of God's love to a needy world.

In the years since those crisis days, I have enjoyed good health, a strong body, and the unexpected gift of four sons. Dr. Titus Johnson wrote reminding me that God had graciously worked a miracle.

Most of us realize the importance of witnessing with love, but the big question is how? How can I possess the gift of love? How can I improve in loving others?

Of course, the source of all love is God Himself. "God is love" (1 John 4:16), and we begin the adventure of love by receiving Jesus Christ and cultivating a knowledge of God. Let me suggest four practical thoughts that have been helpful to me.

MAKE LOVE YOUR AIM

Repeatedly the Bible tells us of the supreme importance of God's love in all that we do. Love is the true motive for all service in Christ's name.

Paul called this divine love "a more excellent way" (1 Corinthians 12:31). Of all the gifts listed in 1 Corinthians 12, love is the greatest. Faith has priority, but love has preeminence. Paul tells us that love supersedes faith and hope (1 Corinthians 13:13). Love is greater than eloquence, the gift of prophecy, knowledge, faith, acts of benevolence, and even martyrdom (1 Corinthians 13:1-3).

John called love the new commandment (John 13:34), and said it was to be the mark that would distinguish us as His disciples. "By this shall all men know that ye are my disciples, if ye have love one to another" (John 13:35). I wonder if our friends and associates sense the love of God in us.

Peter, too, underscored the supremacy of love. "And above all things have fervent [love] among yourselves: for [love] shall cover the multitude of sins" (1 Peter 4:8). Above all that Peter had taught is the importance of God's love.

If love becomes your aim, consciously and subconsciously you will "follow after love" (1 Corinthians 14:1).

When we are aware of the importance of love, it is easier to remember that we must witness with love.

PRAY FOR LOVE

Each day in my devotions, I ask the Lord for a loving spirit. Paul wrote to the Philippians, "And this I pray, that your love may abound yet more and more in knowledge and in all judgment" (Philippians 1:9). Divine love is not soft or sentimental, but aware, alert, and involved. May I challenge you to pray specifically and daily for abounding love, because without it you are nothing and everything else profits nothing (1 Corinthians 13:1, 3).

May I urge you also to realize that God's love is the greatest of all gifts and to make time to pursue it.

LOVE IS A FRUIT

Love is a fruit of the Spirit. Before natural fruit is produced, it is subjected to the elements—sunshine, rain, wind, and plenty of time. Eventually the ripened fruit appears. Paul reminds us that "the fruit of the Spirit is love" (Galatians 5:22). It takes the trials and tears of life, the winds and rains of adversity, and all that God has for us, to produce love as a fruit of the Spirit.

ALLOW THE HOLY SPIRIT TO LOVE THROUGH YOU

Love is not something we work up, but it is allowing the Holy Spirit to love through us. Our natural hearts love self and things. But the secret of loving can be realized when a person permits the Holy Spirit to take control. Listen to Paul, "The love of God is shed abroad in our hearts by the Holy Ghost which is given unto us" (Romans 5:5).

The way to experience the full, overflowing love of God is by yielding to the Holy Spirit. That is the real secret of witnessing with love. I can't but He can. Nothing less than total commitment to Christ will provide this flood of love in your life.

Satan is opposed to faith. He did everything in his power to stop you from receiving Jesus Christ in the first place. And now, after you have received Christ by faith, Satan focuses all his efforts to stop you from growing in faith. What he failed to accomplish before conversion, he often succeeds in after conversion.

At times I have had to love someone by faith and then God stepped in to replace my weak, imperfect feelings with His love. Ask the Lord to give you the ability to love by faith. Some people are hard to love. Recently, a young lady came to me for counsel. As we talked, she poured out a story of hatred and bitterness that she felt toward her parents.

After sharing with her from God's Word, I was able to lead her to accept Christ as her personal Saviour. Almost immediately she said, "I want to be reconciled with my parents, but how can I love them?"

"By faith," I replied. "Go home and believe that God will give you a new love, His love, for your mother and father. He can, and He will!"—and He did.

Real love serves. Love is not content to sit and do nothing. Love is active. It has to express itself in giving, in serving, in witnessing. The proof of our love comes in our willingness to share. A high-school girl who used to criticize people, now sees the selfishness in this practice. She has a God-given desire to understand her friends' shortcomings—as well as her own. She wants to pray for them and share with love.

I do not mean by all this that we must always be on the go. Surely, we must worship before we work; meditation must precede ministering; being tuned in to the Spirit precedes being tuned in to others. There must always be that retirement in which our souls are refreshed and prepared for witnessing.

The early Christians gave themselves to prayer and communion, which in turn resulted in a spontaneous expansion. How much more do we in this jet age need to worship Christ before we can witness for Christ? "They that wait upon the LORD shall renew their strength; they shall mount up with wings like eagles; they shall run, and not be weary; and they shall walk, and not faint" (Isaiah 40:31). When you are yielded to the Holy Spirit, your worship and witness are blended together. Witnessing is the fruit of worshiping. The fullness of love is the natural result of the fullness of the Holy Spirit. *Witnessing begins and ends with love.*

REMINDERS

- Faith has priority, but love has preeminence.
- Love is not something we work up, rather it is allowing the Holy Spirit the chance to love through us.
- The fullness of love is the result of the fullness of the Holy Spirit.
- At times, I have had to love someone by faith, and then God stepped in to transform my weak, imperfect attempt to real love.

QUESTIONS

1. On what subject in this chapter do Paul, Peter, and John agree, and how?
2. Who is the source of all true love and what is the first step in receiving this love?
3. Why is it important to establish God's love as your aim?
4. Is divine love blind sentimentalism? Exactly what did Paul pray for on behalf of the Philippian Christians?
5. What is the secret of the fullness of love?
6. What do we mean by the phrase "loving a person by faith"?

DATE DUE